Congressional
Research Service
Informing the legislative debate since 1914 _____

Medal of Honor Recipients: 1979-2014

Anne Leland

Information Research Specialist

October 29, 2014

Congressional Research Service

7-5700

www.crs.gov

RL30011

Summary

The Medal of Honor (MOH) is the nation's highest award for military valor. It is presented by the President in the name of Congress and is often called the Congressional Medal of Honor. Since its first presentation in 1863, close to 3,500 MOHs have been awarded. In 1973, the Senate Committee on Veterans' Affairs issued a committee print, *Vietnam Era Medal of Honor Recipients 1964-72*, followed by the committee print, *Medal of Honor Recipients: 1863-1978*, in 1979. Both committee prints list recipients and provide the full text of the citation, which describes the actions that resulted in the awarding of the medal.

This report covers additions and changes to the list of recipients of the medal since the release of the committee print. For further information, see CRS Report 95-519, *Medal of Honor: History and Issues*, by David F. Burrelli and Barbara Salazar Torreon.

The official citations are not always consistent in wording for all recipients. Some of the citations do not contain information such as company, division, date of birth, or place of birth. An asterisk (*) indicates those individuals who were awarded their medal posthumously.

This report will be updated as new recipients are named.

Contents

Contacts

Introduction

The Congressional Research Service receives numerous requests for lists of recipients of the Medal of Honor (MOH), the nation's highest award for military bravery. Since its first presentation in 1863, there have been more than 3,400[1] recipients of the Medals of Honor. In 1973 and 1979, the Senate Veterans' Affairs Committee issued Committee Print 8, *Vietnam Era Medal of Honor Recipients: 1964-1972*,[2] and Committee Print 3, *Medal of Honor Recipients: 1863-1978*.[3] Each print lists recipients and provides the full text of the citations describing the actions that resulted in the awarding of the MOH. Since the release of the committee prints, there have been several additions and changes to the list of recipients of this award.

This report continues the work of the above-mentioned committee prints and lists those additions and changes by military action and provides the full text of their official citations. An asterisk (*) indicates those individuals who were awarded their medals posthumously.

> The citations are written in draft form by the time the recommendation packet leaves the hands of the individual's CO (commanding officer). Thus the originator of the citation is whomever the CO has detailed to compile the evidence and eyewitness statements. It's called the "proposed citation" and is a whole section of the form.
>
> As the citation is processed through the chain of command, it is edited. The final citation that is read at the presentation ceremony is a composite work completed by everyone in the chain of command.[4]

Further detailed information about the recommendation process may be found at http://www.army.mil/medalofhonor/process.html.

The citations are published in a Department of the Army general order by the U.S. Army Human Resources Command, Awards and Decorations Branch at http://www.apd.army.mil/AdminPubs/DAGO_by_Year.asp.

The citations are also published by the Department of the Army Center of Military History. Links to additional agencies and Internet sites concerned with awards for valor are provided at the end of this report.

The Congressional Medal of Honor Society (CMOHS) was congressionally chartered[5] and signed into law by President Dwight D. Eisenhower on August 5, 1958, for the purpose of encouraging patriotism and honoring all recipients of the MOH. It contains all MOH citations along with historical information, statistics, and information pertinent to the award. It may be accessed at http://www.cmohs.org.

In some instances, Congress approved legislation to remove statutory time limits in order for the MOH to be awarded. Where this has occurred, the legislation is cited.

---

[1] United States Army, Center of Military History, at http://www history.army.mil/moh/index.html. See also Congressional Medal of Honor Society, at http:cmohs.org/medal-statistics.php.

[2] U.S. Congress, Senate Committee on Veterans' Affairs, *Vietnam Era Medal of Honor Medal of Honor Recipients 1964-1972*, Committee Print 8 (Washington, DC: GPO, 1973).

[3] U.S. Congress, Senate Committee on Veterans' Affairs, *Medal of Honor Recipients 1863-1978*, Committee Print 3 (Washington, DC: GPO, 1979).

[4] Archivist, Congressional Medal of Honor Society, correspondence received July 31, 2012.

[5] P.L. 85-642; 36 U.S.C. §33.

Date of issue information, if not provided by CMOHS or the military branches, was located on the website of Military Times/Home of Heroes at http://www.homeofheroes.com/a_homepage/ community.html or through news reports.

The FY1996 National Defense Authorization Act (P.L. 104-106, Title V, Subtitle C, Section 524) provided for the review of records relating to Asian Americans and Native American Pacific Islanders who received Distinguished Service Crosses or Navy Crosses for service during World War II. This legislation also waived the time limit to allow the President to award the MOH; consequently, 22 Asian Americans received the MOH.

The FY1997 National Defense Authorization Act (P.L. 104-201, Title V, Subtitle G, Sections 561 and 562 September 23, 1996) waived the time limit to allow the President to award the MOH to seven African American soldiers for their heroic acts during World War II. (Some military personnel records were destroyed for these individuals in a 1973 fire at the National Personnel Records Center. Records were reconstructed from auxiliary sources; therefore, the place indicated after the date of birth is the home of record at the time the individual entered the military, and not necessarily the place of birth. Data on the place where the individual entered service is often not available.)

In 2002, through the National Defense Authorization Act for Fiscal Year 2002, Congress requested that the Department of Defense (DOD) review records of veterans who may have been passed over to receive the MOH due to their Jewish or Hispanic heritage from World War II to later periods. Earlier measures provided in the National Defense Authorization Act for Fiscal Year 1997[6] authorized review of the records of African Americans who may have also been eligible for the award. DOD's review resulted in 19 veterans approved to be recipients of the MOH. An additional five were named after a review of recipients of the Distinguished Service Cross. President Obama presented the MOH posthumously to 21 veterans and three living recipients on March 18, 2014.

Most recently, on September 15, 2014, President Obama awarded the MOH to Command Sergeant Major Bennie G. Adkins and Specialist 4 Donald P. Sloat for valorous action in the Vietnam War.

For historical information and a more detailed account of congressional and other efforts to award the MOH, see CRS Report 95-519, *Medal of Honor: History and Issues*, by David F. Burrelli and Barbara Salazar Torreon.

See also the Congressional Medal of Honor Society at http://www.cmohs.org and the Department of Defense Military Awards for Valor site at http://valor.defense.gov/.

Medals of Honor by Action

An asterisk (*) indicates those individuals who were awarded their medals posthumously.

---

[6] P.L. 104-201, Title V, Subtitle G, Sections 561, 562.

Civil War

Smith, Andrew Jackson.*

Congress approved "a bill to authorize the award of the Medal of Honor" to Corporal Smith and others[7] on June 20, 2000, removing the statutory time limit on the award.

Rank and organization: Corporal, U.S. Army, 55th Massachusetts Voluntary Infantry. *Place and date:* Near Boyd's Landing, SC, November 30, 1864. *Entered service at:* unknown. *Born:* September 3, 1842. *Date of issue:* January 31, 2001.

Citation: For conspicuous gallantry and intrepidity at the risk of his life above and beyond the call of duty:

Corporal Andrew Jackson Smith, of Clinton, Illinois, a member of the 55th Massachusetts Voluntary Infantry, distinguished himself on November 30, 1864, by saving his regimental colors, after the color bearer was killed during a bloody charge called the Battle of Honey Hill, South Carolina. In the late afternoon, as the 55th Regiment pursued enemy skirmishers and conducted a running fight, they ran into a swampy area backed by a rise where the Confederate Army awaited. The surrounding woods and thick underbrush impeded infantry movement and artillery support. The 55th and 34th regiments formed columns to advance on the enemy position in a flanking movement. As the Confederates repelled other units, the 55th and 54th regiments continued to move into flanking positions. Forced into a narrow gorge crossing a swamp in the face of the enemy position, the 55th's Color-Sergeant was killed by an exploding shell, and Corporal Smith took the Regimental Colors from his hand and carried them through heavy grape and canister fire. Although half of the officers and a third of the enlisted men engaged in the fight were killed or wounded, Corporal Smith continued to expose himself to enemy fire by carrying the colors throughout the battle. Through his actions, the Regimental Colors of the 55th Infantry Regiment were not lost to the enemy.

Corporal Andrew Jackson Smith's extraordinary valor in the face of deadly enemy fire is in keeping with the highest traditions of military service and reflect great credit upon him, the 55th Regiment, and the United States Army.

Spanish-American War

Roosevelt, Theodore*

Congress approved P.L. 105-371 on November 12, 1998, to authorize and request that the President award the Medal of Honor posthumously to Theodore Roosevelt for action in the attack of San Juan Heights, July 1, 1898. President Clinton initiated an Army review. An Army panel approved the award in June 2000.

Rank and organization: Lieutenant Colonel, U.S. Army, First Cavalry Regiment. *Place and date:* San Juan Heights, Republic of Cuba, July 1, 1898. *Entered service:* Resigned position as Assistant Secretary of the Navy to join Army, May 6, 1898. *Born:* October 27, 1858, New York, NY. *Date of issue:* January 16, 2001.

Citation: For conspicuous gallantry and intrepidity at the risk of his life above and beyond the call of duty.

---

[7] P.L. 106-223.

Lieutenant Colonel Theodore Roosevelt distinguished himself by acts of bravery on 1 July 1898, near Santiago de Cuba, Republic of Cuba, while leading a daring charge up San Juan Hill. Lieutenant Colonel Roosevelt, in total disregard for his personal safety, and accompanied by only four or five men, led a desperate and gallant charge up San Juan Hill, encouraging his troops to continue the assault through withering enemy fire over open countryside. Facing the enemy's heavy fire, he displayed extraordinary bravery throughout the charge and was the first to reach the enemy trenches, where he quickly killed one of the enemies with his pistol, allowing his men to continue the assault. His leadership and valor turned the tide in the Battle for San Juan Hill.

Lieutenant Colonel Roosevelt's extraordinary heroism and devotion to duty are in keeping with the highest traditions of military service and reflect great credit upon himself, his unit, and the United States Army.

World War I

Stowers, Freddie*

Corporal Stowers's recommendation was delayed due to administrative error. The law provides that in such cases time limitations may be waived.[8]

Rank and organization: Corporal, U.S. Army, Company C, 371st Infantry Regiment, 93rd Infantry Division. *Place and date:* Champagne Marne Sector, France, September 28, 1918. *Entered service at:* unknown. *Born:* 1897, Anderson County, SC. *Date of issue:* April 24, 1991.

Citation: Corporal Stowers distinguished himself by exceptional heroism on September 28, 1918, while serving as a squad leader in Company C, 371st Infantry Regiment, 93rd Infantry Division.

His company was the lead company during the attack on Hill 188, Champagne Marne Sector, France, during World War I. A few minutes after the attack began, the enemy ceased firing and began climbing up onto the parapets of the trenches, holding up their arms as if wishing to surrender. The enemy's actions caused the American forces to cease fire and to come out into the open. As the company started forward and when within about 100 meters of the trench line, the enemy jumped back into their trenches and greeted Corporal Stowers's company with interlocking bands of machine gun fire and mortar fire causing well over 50% casualties. Faced with incredible enemy resistance, Corporal Stowers took charge, setting such a courageous example of personal bravery and leadership that he inspired his men to follow him in the attack. With extraordinary heroism and complete disregard of personal danger under devastating fire, he crawled forward leading his squad toward an enemy machine gun nest, which was causing heavy casualties to his company. After fierce fighting, the machine gun position was destroyed and the enemy soldiers were killed. Displaying great courage and intrepidity, Corporal Stowers continued to press the attack against a determined enemy. While crawling forward and urging his men to continue the attack on a second trench line, he was gravely wounded by machine gun fire. Although Corporal Stowers was mortally wounded, he pressed forward, urging on the members of his squad until he died. Inspired by the heroism and display of bravery of Corporal Stowers, his company continued the attack against incredible odds, contributing to the capture of Hill 188 and causing heavy enemy casualties.

---

[8] 10 U.S.C. §3744, 6248, 8744.

Corporal Stowers's conspicuous gallantry, extraordinary heroism, and supreme devotion to his men were well above and beyond the call of duty, follow the finest traditions of military service, and reflect the utmost credit on him and the United States Army.

World War II

Baker, Vernon J.

Lieutenant Baker was among the seven African Americans who were awarded the MOH for their heroic acts during World War II following Congress's approval of P.L. 104-201, which waived the time limit to allow the President to award the MOH.

Rank and organization: First Lieutenant, U.S. Army, Company C, 370th Infantry Regiment. *Place and date:* Near Viareggio, Italy, April 5 and 6, 1945. *Entered service:* June 26, 1941. *Born:* December 17, 1919, Cheyenne, WY. *Date of issue:* January 13, 1997.

Citation: For extraordinary heroism in action on April 5 and 6, 1945, near Viareggio, Italy. Then-Second Lieutenant Baker demonstrated outstanding courage and leadership in destroying enemy installations, personnel, and equipment during his company's attack against a strongly entrenched enemy in mountainous terrain. When his company was stopped by the concentration of fire from several machine gun emplacements, he crawled to one position and destroyed it, killing three Germans. Continuing forward, he attacked and enemy observation post and killed two occupants. With the aid of one of his men, Lieutenant Baker attacked two more machine gun nests, killing or wounding the four enemy soldiers occupying these positions. He then covered the evacuation of the wounded personnel of his company by occupying an exposed position and drawing the enemy's fire. On the following night Lieutenant Baker voluntarily led a battalion advance through enemy mine fields and heavy fire toward the division objective. Second Lieutenant Baker's fighting spirit and daring leadership were an inspiration to his men and exemplify the highest traditions of the Armed Forces.

Cano, Pedro

Private Cano's military records military records were reviewed under the FY2002 National Defense Authorization Act, in which Congress requested that the DOD review service records of certain Jewish Americans or Hispanic Americans who had been awarded the Distinguished Service Cross, Navy Cross, or Air Force Cross.

Rank and organization: Private, 4th Infantry Division, U.S. Army. *Place and date:* Schevenhütte, Germany, December 2-3, 1944. *Entered service at:* Texas. *Born:* June 19, 1920, La Morita, Mexico. *Date of issue:* March 18, 2014.

Citation: For conspicuous gallantry and intrepidity at the risk of his life above and beyond the call of duty:

Private Pedro Cano distinguished himself by acts of gallantry and intrepidity above and beyond the call of duty while serving with Company C, 8th Infantry Regiment, 4th Infantry Division during combat operations against an armed enemy in Schevenhütte, Germany on December 2 and 3, 1944. On the afternoon of the 2nd, American infantrymen launched an attack against German emplacements but were repulsed by enemy machinegun fire. Armed with a rocket launcher, Private Cano crawled through a densely mined area under heavy enemy fire and successfully reached a point within 10 yards of the nearest emplacement. He quickly fired a rocket into the position, killing the two gunners and five supporting riflemen. Without hesitating, he fired into a second position, killing two more gunners, and proceeded to assault the position with hand grenades, killing several others and dispersing the rest. Then, when an adjacent company encountered heavy fire, Private Cano crossed his company front, crept to within 15 yards of the nearest enemy emplacement, and killed the two machinegunners with a rocket. With another round he killed two more gunners and destroyed a second gun. On the following day, his company renewed the attack and again encountered heavy machinegun fire. Private Cano, armed with his rocket launcher, again moved across fire-swept terrain and destroyed three enemy machineguns in succession, killing the six gunners. Private Cano's extraordinary heroism and selflessness above and beyond the call of duty are in keeping with the highest traditions of military service and reflect great credit upon himself, his unit, and the United States Army.

Carter, Edward A., Jr.*

Sergeant Carter was among the seven African Americans who were awarded the MOH for their heroic acts during World War II following Congress's approval of P.L. 104-201, which waived the time limit to allow the President to award the MOH.

Rank and Organization: Staff Sergeant, Seventh Army Infantry Company Number 1 (Provisional), U.S. Army. *Place and date:* Near Speyer, Germany, 23 March 1945. *Entered service:* September 26, 1941. *Born:* May 26, 1916, Los Angeles, CA. *Date of issue:* January 13, 1997.

Citation: Staff Sergeant Edward A. Carter, Jr. distinguished himself by extraordinary heroism in action on March 23, 1945.

For extraordinary heroism in action on March 23, 1945, near Speyer, Germany. When the tank on which he was riding received heavy bazooka and small arms fire, Sergeant Carter voluntarily attempted to lead a three-man group across an open field. Within a short time, two of his men were killed and the third seriously wounded. Continuing on alone, he was wounded five times and finally forced to take cover. As eight enemy riflemen attempted to capture him, Sergeant Carter killed six of them and captured the remaining two. He then crossed the field using as a shield his two prisoners from which he obtained valuable information concerning the disposition of enemy troops. Staff Sergeant Carter's extraordinary heroism was an inspiration to the officers and men of the Seventh Army Infantry Company Number 1 (Provisional) and exemplify the highest traditions of the Armed Forces.

Casamento, Anthony

Congress approved P.L. 95-163 on November 2, 1977, removing the statutory time limit on the award for Corporal Casamento.

Rank and organization: Corporal, Company "D," First Battalion, Fifth Marines, First Marine Division, U.S. Marine Corps. *Place and date:* Guadalcanal, November 1, 1942. *Entered service at:* Brooklyn, NY, August 19, 1940. *Born:* November 16, 1920, Brooklyn, NY. *Date of issue:* September 12, 1980.[9]

Citation: For conspicuous gallantry and intrepidity at the risk of his life above and beyond the call of duty while serving with Company "D," First Battalion, Fifth Marines, First Marine Division on Guadalcanal, British Solomon Islands, in action against the enemy Japanese forces on November 1,1942.

---

[9] *New York Times*, "Ex-Marine Wins Long Battle," September 13, 1980.

Serving as a leader of a machine gun section, Corporal Casamento directed his unit to advance along a ridge near the Mantanikau River where they engaged the enemy. He positioned his section to provide covering fire for two flanking units and to provide direct support for the main force of his company, which was behind him. During the course of this engagement, all members of his section were either killed or severely wounded and he himself suffered multiple, grievous wounds. Nonetheless, Corporal Casamento continued to provide critical supporting fire for the attack and in defense of his position. Following the loss of all effective personnel, he set up, loaded, and manned his unit's machine gun, tenaciously holding the enemy forces at bay. Corporal Casamento single-handedly engaged and destroyed one machine gun emplacement to his front and took under fire the other emplacement on the flank. Despite the heat and ferocity of the engagement, he continued to man his weapon and repeatedly repulsed multiple assaults by the enemy forces, thereby protecting the flanks of the adjoining companies and holding his position until the arrival of his main attacking force. Corporal Casamento's courageous fighting spirit, heroic conduct, and unwavering dedication to duty reflected great credit upon himself and were in keeping with the highest traditions of the Marine Corps and the United States Naval Service.

Davila, Rudolph B.

Staff Sergeant Davila's military records were among those reviewed under the FY1996 National Defense Authorization Act (P.L. 104-106, Section 524). Following review, he was awarded the MOH.

Rank and organization: Staff Sergeant, Company H, 7th Infantry, U.S. Army. *Place and date:* Near Artena, Italy, March 28, 1944. *Entered service:* March 6, 1941 *Born:* April 27, 1916, El Paso, Texas. *Date of issue:* June 21, 2000.

Citation: For conspicuous gallantry and intrepidity at the risk of his life above and beyond the call of duty:

Staff Sergeant Rudolph B. Davila distinguished himself by extraordinary heroism in action, on May 28, 1944, near Artena, Italy. During the offensive which broke through the German mountain strongholds surrounding the Anzio beachhead, Staff Sergeant Davila risked death to provide heavy weapons support for a beleaguered rifle company. Caught on an exposed hillside by heavy, grazing fire from a well-entrenched German force, his machine gunners were reluctant to risk putting their guns into action. Crawling fifty yard to the nearest machine gun, Staff Sergeant Davila set it up alone and opened fire on the enemy. In order to observe the effect of his fire, Sergeant Davila fired from the kneeling position, ignoring the enemy fire that struck the tripod and passed between his legs. Ordering a gunner to take over, he crawled forward to a vantage point and directed the fire fight with hand and arm signals until both hostile machine guns were silenced. Bringing his three remaining machine guns into action, he drove the enemy to a reserve position two hundred yards to the rear. When he received a painful wound in the leg, he dashed to a burned tank and, despite the crash of bullets on the hull, engaged a second enemy force from the tank's turret. Dismounting, he advanced 130 yards in short rushes, crawled 20 yards and charged into an enemy-held house to eliminate the defending force of five with a hand grenade and rifle fire. Climbing to the attic, he straddled a large shell hole in the wall and opened fire on the enemy. Although the walls of the house were crumbling, he continued to fire until he had destroyed two more machine guns. His intrepid actions brought desperately needed heavy weapons support to a hard-pressed rifle company and silenced four machine gunners, which forced the enemy to abandon their prepared positions.

Staff Sergeant Davila's extraordinary heroism and devotion to duty are in keeping with the highest traditions of military service and reflect great credit on him, his unit, and the United States Army.

Day, James L.

Corporal Day's recommendation was delayed due to administrative error. The law provides that in such cases time limitations may be waived.[10]

Rank and organization: Corporal, Company "G" Second Battalion, 22nd Marines, Sixth Marine Division. *Place and date:* Okinawa, Ryukyu Islands, May 14-17, 1945. *Entered service:* St. Louis, MO, 1943. Born: October 5, 1925, East St. Louis, IL. *Date of issue:* January 20, 1998.

Citation: For conspicuous gallantry and intrepidity at the risk of his life above and beyond the call of duty as a squad leader serving with the Second Battalion, 22nd Marines, Sixth Marine Division in sustained combat operations against Japanese Forces on Okinawa, Ryukyu Islands, from May 14-17, 1945.

On the first day, Corporal Day rallied his squad and the remnants of another unit and led them to a critical position forward of the front lines of Sugar Loaf Hill. Soon thereafter, they came under an intense mortar and artillery barrage that was quickly followed by a ferocious ground attack by some 40 Japanese soldiers. Despite the loss of one-half of his men, Corporal Day remained at the forefront, shouting encouragement, hurling hand grenades, and directing deadly fire, thereby repelling the determined enemy. Reinforced by six men, he led his squad in repelling three fierce night attacks, but suffered five additional Marines killed and one wounded, whom he assisted to safety. Upon hearing nearby calls for corpsmen assistance, Corporal Day braved heavy enemy fire to escort four seriously wounded Marines, one at a time, to safety. Corporal Day then manned a light machine gun, assisted by a wounded Marine, and halted another night attack. In this ferocious action, his machine gun was destroyed, and he suffered multiple white phosphorous and fragmentation wounds. He reorganized his defensive position in time to halt a fifth enemy attack with devastating small arms fire. On three separate occasions, Japanese soldiers closed to within a few feet of his foxhole, but they were killed by Corporal Day. During the second day, the enemy conducted numerous unsuccessful swarming attacks against his exposed position. When the attacks momentarily subsided, over 70 enemy dead were counted around his position. On the third day, a wounded and exhausted Corporal Day repulsed the enemy's final attack, killing a dozen enemy soldiers at close range. Having yielded no ground and with more than 100 enemy dead around his position, Corporal Day preserved the lives of his fellow Marines and made a significant contribution to the success of the Okinawa campaign.

By his extraordinary heroism, repeated acts of valor and quintessential battle field leadership, Corporal Day inspired the efforts of his outnumbered Marines to defeat a much larger enemy force, reflecting great credit upon himself in upholding the highest standards and traditions of the Marine Corps and United States Naval Service.

Fox, John R.*

Lieutenant Fox was among the seven African Americans who were awarded the MOH for their heroic acts during World War II, following Congress's approval of P.L. 104-201, which waived the time limit to allow the President to award the MOH.

---

[10] 10 U.S.C. §3744, 6248, 8744.

Rank and organization: First Lieutenant, U.S. Army, Cannon Company, 366th Infantry, 92nd Infantry Division, 598th Field Artillery Battalion. *Place and date:* Near Sommocolonia, Italy. *Entered service:* February 28, 1941. *Born:* May 18, 1915, Cincinnati, OH. *Date of issue:* January 13, 1997.

Citation: First Lieutenant John R. Fox distinguished himself by extraordinary heroism at the risk of his own life on 26 December 1944 in the Serchio River Valley Sector, in the vicinity of Sommocolonia, Italy.

Lieutenant Fox was a member of Cannon Company, 366th Infantry, 92nd Infantry Division, acting as a forward observer, while attached to the 598th Field Artillery Battalion. Christmas Day in the Serchio Valley was spent in positions which had been occupied for some weeks. During Christmas night, there was a gradual influx of enemy soldiers in civilian clothes, and by early morning the town was largely in enemy hands. An organized attack by uniformed German formations was launched around 0400 hours, 26 December 1944. Reports were received that the area was being heavily shelled by everything the Germans had, and although most of the U.S. infantry forces withdrew from the town, Lieutenant Fox and members of his observer party remained behind on the second floor of a house, directing defensive fires. Lieutenant Fox reported at 0800 hours that the Germans were in the streets and attacking in strength. He called for artillery fire increasingly close to his own position. He told his battalion commander, "That was just where I wanted it. Bring it in 60 yards!" His commander protested that there was a heavy barrage in the area and the bombardment would be too close. Lieutenant Fox gave his adjustment, requesting that the barrage be fired. The distance was cut in half. The Germans continued to press forward in large numbers, surrounding the position. Lieutenant Fox again called for artillery fire with the commander protesting again stating, "Fox, that will be on you!" The last communication from Lieutenant Fox was "Fire It! There's more of them than there are of us. Give them hell!" The bodies of Lieutenant Fox and his party were found in the vicinity of his position when his position was retaken. This action by Lieutenant Fox, at the cost of his own life, inflicted heavy casualties, causing the deaths of approximately 100 German soldiers, thereby delaying the advance of the enemy until infantry and artillery units could be reorganized to meet the attack.

Lieutenant Fox's extraordinarily valorous actions exemplify the highest traditions of the military service.

Gandara, Joe*

Private Gandara's military records were reviewed under the FY2002 National Defense Authorization Act, in which Congress requested that the DOD review service records of certain Jewish Americans or Hispanic Americans who had been awarded the Distinguished Service Cross, Navy Cross, or Air Force Cross.

Rank and organization: Private, Company D, 2[d] Battalion, 507th Parachute Infantry Regiment, 17th Airborne Division, U.S. Army. *Place and date:* Amfreville, France, June 9, 1944. *Entered service at:* Los Angeles, CA. *Born:* April 25, 1924, Santa Monica, CA. *Date of issue:* March 18, 2014.

Citation: For conspicuous gallantry and intrepidity at the risk of his life above and beyond the call of duty:

Private Joe Gandara distinguished himself by acts of gallantry and intrepidity above and beyond the call of duty while serving with Company D, 2nd Battalion, 507th Parachute Infantry Regiment, 17th Airborne Division during combat operations against an armed enemy in Amfreville, France, on June 9, 1944. On that day, Private Gandara's detachment came under devastating enemy fire from a strong German force, pinning the men to the ground for a period of four hours. Private Gandara voluntarily advanced alone toward the enemy position. Firing his machinegun from his hip as he moved forward, he destroyed three hostile machineguns before he was fatally wounded. Private Gandara's extraordinary heroism and selflessness at the cost of his own life, above and beyond the call of duty, are in keeping with the highest traditions of military service and reflect great credit upon himself, his unit, and the United States Army.

Hajiro, Barney F.

Private Hajiro's military records were among those reviewed under the FY1996 National Defense Authorization Act (P.L. 104-106, Section 524). Following review, he was awarded the MOH.

Rank and organization: Private, U.S. Army, Company I, 442nd Regimental Combat Team. *Place and date:* Near Bruyeres and Biffontaine, France, October 19, 22, 29, 1944. *Entered service at:* Honolulu, HI, 1 February 1942. *Born:* unknown. *Date of issue:* June 21, 2000.

Citation: For conspicuous gallantry and intrepidity at the risk of his life above and beyond the call of duty.

Private Barney F. Hajiro distinguished himself by extraordinary heroism in action on October 19, 22, and 29, 1944, in the vicinity of Bruyeres and Biffontaine, eastern France. Private Hajiro, while acting as a sentry on top of an embankment on October 19, 1944 in the vicinity of Bruyeres, France, rendered assistance to allied troops attacking a house 2000 yards away, exposing himself to enemy fire and directing fire at an enemy strong point. He assisted the unit on his right by firing his automatic rifle and killing or wounding two enemy snipers. On October 22, 1944, he and one comrade took up an outpost security position about 50 yards to the right front of their platoon, concealed themselves, and ambushed an 18-man, heavily armed enemy patrol, killing two, wounding one, and taking the remainder as prisoners. On October 29, 1944, in a wooded area in the vicinity of Biffontaine, France, Private Hajiro initiated an attack up the slope of a hill referred to as "Suicide Hill" by running forward approximately 100 yards under fire. He then advanced ahead of these comrades about 10 yards, drawing fire and spotting camouflaged machine gun nests. He fearlessly met fire with fire and single-handedly destroyed two machine gun nests and killed two enemy snipers. As a result of Private Hajiro's heroic actions, the attack was successful.

Private Hajiro's extraordinary heroism and devotion to duty are in keeping with the highest traditions of military service and reflect great credit upon him, his unit, and the United States Army.

Hasemoto, Miko*

Private Hasemoto's military records were among those reviewed under the FY1996 National Defense Authorization Act (P.L. 104-106, Section 524). Following review, he was awarded the MOH.

Rank and organization: Private, U.S. Army, Company B, 100th Infantry Battalion, 34th Infantry Division. *Place and date:* Near Cerasuolo, Italy, 29 November 1943. *Entered service at:* Schofield Barracks, HI, 30 June 1941. *Born:* 16 July 1916, Honolulu, HI. *Date of issue:* June 21, 2000.

Citation. For conspicuous gallantry and intrepidity at the risk of his life above and beyond the call of duty:

Private Mikio Hasemoto distinguished himself by extraordinary heroism in action on 29 November 1943, in the vicinity of Cerasuolo, Italy. A force of approximately 40 enemy soldiers, armed with machine guns, machine pistols, rifles, and grenades, attacked the left flank of the platoon. Two enemy soldiers with machine guns advanced forward, firing their weapons. Private Hasemoto, an automatic rifleman, challenged these two machine gunners. After firing four magazines at the approaching enemy, his weapon was shot and damaged. Unhesitatingly, he ran 10 yards to the rear, secured another automatic rifle and continued to fire until his weapon jammed. At this point, Private Hasemoto and his squad leader had killed approximately 20 enemy soldiers. Again, Private Hasemoto ran through a barrage of enemy machine gun fire to pick up an M-1 rifle. Continuing their fire, Private Hasemoto and his squad leader killed 10 more enemy soldiers. With only three enemy soldiers left, he and his squad leader charged courageously forward, killing one, wounding one, and capturing another. The following day, Private Hasemoto continued to repel enemy attacks until he was killed by enemy fire.

Private Hasemoto's extraordinary heroism and devotion to duty are in keeping with the highest traditions of military service and reflect great credit on him, his unit, and the United States Army.

Hayashi, Joe*

Private Hayashi's military records were among those reviewed under the FY1996 National Defense Authorization Act (P.L. 104-106, Section 524). Following review, he was awarded the MOH.

Rank and organization: Private, U.S. Army, Company K, 442nd Regimental Combat Team. *Place and date:* Near Tendola, Italy, 20 and 22 April 1945. *Entered service:* unknown. *Born:* circa 1919. *Date of issue:* June 21, 2000.

Citation: For conspicuous gallantry and intrepidity at the risk of his life above and beyond the call of duty:

Private Joe Hayashi distinguished himself by extraordinary heroism in action on 20 and 22 April 1945, near Tendola, Italy. On 20 April 1945, ordered to attack a strongly defended hill that commanded all approaches to the village of Tendola, Private Hayashi skillfully led his men to a point within 75 yards of enemy positions before they were detected and fired upon. After dragging his wounded comrades to safety, he returned alone and exposed himself to small arms fire in order to direct and adjust mortar fire against hostile emplacements. Boldly attacking the hill with the remaining men of his squad, he attained his objective and discovered that the mortars had neutralized three machine guns, killed 27 men, and wounded many others. On 22 April 1945, attacking the village of Tendola, Private Hayashi maneuvered his squad up a steep, terraced hill to within 100 yards of the enemy. Crawling under intense fire to a hostile machine gun position, he threw a grenade, killing one enemy soldier and forcing the other members of the gun crew to surrender. Seeing four enemy machine guns delivering deadly fire upon other elements of his platoon, he threw another grenade, destroying a machine gun nest. He then crawled to the right flank of another machine gun position where he killed four enemy soldiers and forced the others to flee. Attempting to pursue the enemy, he was mortally wounded by a burst of machine pistol fire. The dauntless courage and exemplary leadership of Private Hayashi enabled his company to attain its objective.

Private Hayashi's extraordinary heroism and devotion to duty are in keeping with the highest traditions of military service and reflect great credit on him, his unit and the United States Army.

Hayashi, Shizuya

Private Hayashi's military records were among those reviewed under the FY1996 National Defense Authorization Act (P.L. 104-106, Section 524). Following review, he was awarded the MOH.

Rank and organization: Private, U.S. Army, Company A, 100th Battalion (Separate), 34th Infantry Division. *Place and date:* Near Cerasuolo, Italy, 29 November 1943. *Entered service:* Schofield Barracks, HI, 24 March 1941. *Born:* 28 November 1917, Waialua (Oahu), HI. *Date of issue:* June 21, 2000.

Citation: For conspicuous gallantry and intrepidity at the risk of his life above and beyond the call of duty.

Private Shizuya Hayashi distinguished himself by extraordinary heroism in action on 29 November 1943, near Cerasuolo, Italy. During a flank assault on high ground held by the enemy, Private Hayashi rose alone in the face of grenade, rifle, and machine gun fire. Firing his automatic rifle from the hip, he charged and overtook an enemy machine gun position, killing seven men in the nest and two more as they fled. After his platoon advanced 200 yards from this point, an enemy antiaircraft gun opened fire on the men. Private Hayashi returned fire at the hostile position, killing nine of the enemy, taking four prisoners, and forcing the remainder of the force to withdraw from the hill.

Private Hayashi's extraordinary heroism and devotion to duty are in keeping with the highest traditions of military service and reflect great credit on him, his unit, and the United States Army.

Inouye, Daniel K.

Mr. Inouye's military records military records were among those reviewed under the FY1996 National Defense Authorization Act (P.L. 104-106, Section 524). Following review, he was awarded the MOH.

Rank and organization: Second Lieutenant, U.S. Army, Company E, 442nd Infantry Regiment. *Place and date:* Near San Terenzo, Italy, 21 April 1945. *Entered service at:* Honolulu, HI, 5 November 1944. *Born:* 7 September 1924, Honolulu, HI. *Date of issue:* June 21, 2000.

Citation: For conspicuous gallantry and intrepidity at the risk of his life above and beyond the call of duty:

Second Lieutenant Daniel K. Inouye distinguished himself by extraordinary heroism in action on 21 April 1945, in the vicinity of San Terenzo, Italy. While attacking a defended ridge guarding an important road junction, Second Lieutenant Inouye skillfully directed his platoon through a hail of automatic weapon and small arms fire, in a swift enveloping movement that resulted in the capture of an artillery and mortar post and brought his men to within 40 yards of the hostile force. Emplaced in bunkers and rock formations, the enemy halted the advance with crossfire from three machine guns. With complete disregard for his personal safety, Second Lieutenant Inouye crawled up the treacherous slope to within five yards of the nearest machine gun and hurled two grenades, destroying the emplacement. Before the enemy could retaliate, he stood up and neutralized a second machine gun nest. Although wounded by a sniper's bullet, he continued to engage other hostile positions at close range until an exploding grenade shattered his right arm. Despite the intense pain, he refused evacuation and continued to direct his platoon until enemy resistance was broken and his men were again deployed in defensive positions. In the attack, 25 enemy soldiers were killed and eight others captured. By his gallant, aggressive tactics and by his indomitable leadership, Second Lieutenant Inouye enabled his platoon to advance through formidable resistance and was instrumental in the capture of the ridge.

Second Lieutenant Inouye's extraordinary heroism and devotion to duty are in keeping with the highest traditions of military service and reflect great credit on him, his unit, and the United States Army.

James, Willy F., Jr.*

Private James was among the seven African Americans who were awarded the MOH for their heroic acts during World War II, following Congress's approval of P.L. 104-201, which waived the time limit to allow the President to award the MOH.

Rank and organization: Private First Class, U.S. Army, Company G, 413th Infantry. *Place and date:* Near Lippoldsberg, Germany, April 7, 1945. *Entered service:* September 11, 1942. *Born:* March 18, 1920, Kansas City, MO. *Date of issue:* January 13, 1997.

Citation: Private First Class Willy F. James, Jr. distinguished himself by extraordinary heroism at the risk of his own life on 7 April 1945 in the Weser River Valley, in the vicinity of Lippoldsberg, Germany.

On April 7, 1945, Company G, 413th Infantry, fought its way across the Weser River in order to establish a crucial bridgehead. The company then launched a fierce attack against the town of Lippoldsberg, possession of which was vital to securing and expanding the important bridgehead. Private First Class James was first scout of the lead squad in the assault platoon. The mission of the unit was to seize and secure a group of houses on the edge of town, a foothold from which the unit could launch an attack on the rest of the town. Far out in the front, Private First Class James was the first to draw enemy fire. His platoon leader came forward to investigate, but poor visibility made it difficult for Private First Class James to point out enemy positions with any accuracy. Private First Class James volunteered to go forward to fully reconnoiter the enemy situation. Furious crossfire from enemy snipers and machine guns finally pinned down Private First Class James after he had made his way forward approximately 200 yards across open terrain. Lying in an exposed position for more than an hour, Private First Class James intrepidly observed the enemy's positions, which were given away by the fire he was daringly drawing upon himself. Then, with utter indifference to his personal safety, in a storm of enemy small arms fire, Private First Class James made his way back more than 300 yards across open terrain under enemy observation to his platoon positions, and gave a full detailed report on the enemy disposition. The unit worked out a new plan of maneuver based on Private First Class James's information. The gallant soldier volunteered to lead a squad in an assault on the key house in the group that formed the platoon objective. He made his way forward, leading his squad in an assault on the strongly held enemy positions in the building and designating targets accurately and continuously as he moved along. While doing so, Private First Class James saw his platoon leader shot down by enemy snipers. Hastily designating and coolly orienting a leader in his place, Private First Class James instantly went to the aid of his platoon leader, exposing himself recklessly to the incessant enemy fire. As he was making his way across open ground, Private First Class James was killed by a burst from an enemy machine gun. Private First Class James's extraordinarily heroic action in the face of withering enemy fire provided the disposition of enemy troops to his platoon. Inspired to the utmost by Private First Class James's self-sacrifice, the platoon sustained the momentum of the assault and successfully accomplished its mission with a minimum of casualties. Private First Class James contributed very definitely to the success of his battalion in the vitally important combat operation of establishing and expanding a bridgehead over the Weser River.

His fearless, self-assigned actions far above and beyond the normal call of duty exemplify the finest traditions of the American combat soldier and reflect the highest credit upon Private First Class James and the Armed Forces of the United States.

Kobashigawa, Yeiki

Sergeant Kobashigawa's military records were among those reviewed under the FY1996 National Defense Authorization Act (P.L. 104-106, Section 524). Following review, he was awarded the MOH.

Rank and organization: Technical Sergeant, U.S. Army, Company B, 100th Infantry Battalion (Separate), 34th Infantry Division. *Place and date:* Near Lanuvio Italy, 2 June 1944. *Entered service at:* Honolulu, HI, 14 November 1941. *Born:* 28 September 1917, Hilo, HI. *Date of issue:* June 21, 2000.

Citation: For conspicuous gallantry and intrepidity at the risk of his life above and beyond the call of duty:

Technical Sergeant Yeiki Kobashigawa distinguished himself by extraordinary heroism in action on 2 June 1944, in the vicinity of Lanuvio Italy. During an attack, Technical Sergeant Kobashigawa's platoon encountered strong enemy resistance from a series of machine guns providing supporting fire. Observing a machine gun nest 50 yards from his position, Technical Sergeant Kobashigawa crawled forward with one of his men, threw a grenade and then charged the enemy with his submachine gun while a fellow soldier provided covering fire. He killed one enemy soldier and captured two prisoners. Meanwhile, Technical Sergeant Kobashigawa and his comrade were fired upon by another machine gun 50 yards ahead. Directing a squad to advance to his first position, the Technical Sergeant Kobashigawa again moved forward with a fellow soldier to subdue the second machine gun nest. After throwing grenades into the position, Technical Sergeant Kobashigawa provided close supporting fire while a fellow soldier charged, capturing four prisoners. On the alert for other machine gun nests, Technical Sergeant Kobashigawa discovered four more, and skillfully led a squad in neutralizing two of them.

Technical Sergeant Kobashigawa's extraordinary heroism and devotion to duty are in keeping with the highest traditions of military service and reflect great credit on him, his unit, and the United States Army.

Kuroda, Robert T.*

Sergeant Kuroda's military records were among those reviewed under the FY1996 National Defense Authorization Act (P.L. 104-106, Section 524). Following review, he was awarded the Medal of Honor.

Rank and organization: Staff Sergeant, U.S. Army, Company H, 442nd Regimental Combat Team. *Place and date:* Near Bruyeres, France, 20 October 1944. *Entered service:* March 23 , 1943. *Born:* November 8, 1922. *Date of issue:* June 21, 2000.

Citation: For conspicuous gallantry and intrepidity at the risk of his life above and beyond the call of duty:

Staff Sergeant Robert T. Kuroda distinguished himself by extraordinary heroism in action, on 20 October 1944, near Bruyeres, France. Leading his men in an advance to destroy snipers and machine gun nests, Staff Sergeant Kuroda encountered heavy fire from enemy soldiers occupying a heavily wooded slope. Unable to pinpoint the hostile machine gun, he boldly made his way through heavy fire to the crest of the ridge. Once he located the machine gun, Staff Sergeant

Kuroda advanced to a point within 10 yards of the nest and killed three enemy gunners with grenades. He then fired clip after clip of rifle ammunition, killing or wounding at least three of the enemy. As he expended the last of his ammunition, he observed that an American officer had been struck by a burst of fire from a hostile machine gun located on an adjacent hill. Rushing to the officer's assistance, he found that the officer had been killed. Picking up the officer's submachine gun, Staff Sergeant Kuroda advanced through continuous fire toward a second machine gun emplacement and destroyed the position. As he turned to fire upon additional enemy soldiers, he was killed by a sniper. Staff Sergeant Kuroda's courageous actions and indomitable fighting spirit ensured the destruction of enemy resistance in the sector.

Staff Sergeant Kuroda's extraordinary heroism and devotion to duty are in keeping with the highest traditions of military service and reflect great credit on him, his unit, and the United States Army.

Lara, Salvador J.*

Private Lara's military records were reviewed under the FY2002 National Defense Authorization Act, in which Congress requested that the DOD review service records of certain Jewish Americans or Hispanic Americans who had been awarded the Distinguished Service Cross, Navy Cross, or Air Force Cross.

Rank and organization: Private First Class, Company L, 180th Infantry, 45th Infantry Division, U.S. Army. *Place and date:* Aprilia, Italy, May 27-28, 1944. *Entered service at:* Riverside, CA. *Born:* 1920. *Date of issue:* March 18, 2014.

Citation: For conspicuous gallantry and intrepidity at the risk of his life above and beyond the call of duty:

Private First Class Salvador J. Lara distinguished himself by acts of gallantry and intrepidity above and beyond the call of duty while serving as the squad leader of a rifle squad with 2nd Platoon, Company L, 180th Infantry, 45th Infantry Division during combat operations against an armed enemy in Aprilia, Italy, on May 27 and 28, 1944. On the afternoon of the 27th, Private First Class Lara aggressively led his rifle squad in neutralizing multiple enemy strongpoints and in inflicting large numbers of casualties on the enemy. Having taken his initial objective, Private First Class Lara noticed that the unit to his right was meeting stiff resistance from a large, well-entrenched enemy force in a deep ditch. Private First Class Lara quickly gathered three men and attacked a wide section of the enemy position, killing four, forcing 15 others to surrender, and causing two enemy mortar crews to abandon their weapons. His fearless and efficient performance enabled both his own unit and the unit to his right to continue to their objective. The next morning, as his company resumed the attack, Private First Class Lara sustained a severe leg wound, but did not stop to receive first aid. His company suffered heavy casualties as a result of withering machinegun fire coming from an enemy strongpoint on the right flank. After requesting permission to destroy the enemy machineguns armed only with a Browning automatic rifle, Private First Class Lara crawled alone toward the nearest machinegun. Despite his painful wound and the extreme danger of the task, he rose and fearlessly charged the nest, killing the crew members. Another machinegun opened fire on him, but he quickly neutralized this weapon with accurate fire from his Browning, killing three more of the enemy. His aggressive attack forced two other machinegun crews to flee their weapons. After rejoining his company, Private First Class Lara continued his exemplary performance until he captured his objective. Private First Class Lara's extraordinary heroism and selflessness above and beyond the call of duty are in keeping with the highest traditions of military service and reflect great credit upon himself, his unit, and the United States Army.

Leonard, William F.*

Private Leonard's military records were reviewed under the FY2002 National Defense Authorization Act, in which Congress requested that the DOD review service records of certain Jewish Americans or Hispanic Americans who had been awarded the Distinguished Service Cross, Navy Cross, or Air Force Cross.

Rank and organization: Private First Class, Company C, 30th Infantry Regiment, U.S. Army. *Place and date:* St. Die, France, November 7, 1944. *Entered service at:* Lockport, NJ. *Born:* August 9, 1913, Lockport, NJ. *Date of issue:* March 18, 2014.

Citation: For conspicuous gallantry and intrepidity at the risk of his life above and beyond the call of duty:

Private First Class William F. Leonard distinguished himself by acts of gallantry and intrepidity above and beyond the call of duty while serving as a squad leader in Company C, 30th Infantry Regiment, 3rd Infantry Division during combat operations against an armed enemy near St. Die, France, on November 7, 1944. Private First Class Leonard's platoon was reduced to eight men as a result of blistering artillery, mortar, machinegun, and rifle fire. Private First Class Leonard led the survivors in an assault over a hill covered by trees and shrubs that the enemy continuously swept with automatic weapons fire. Ignoring bullets that pierced his pack, Private First Class Leonard killed two snipers at ranges of 50 and 75 yards and engaged and destroyed a machinegun nest with grenades, killing its two-man crew. Though momentarily stunned by an exploding bazooka shell, Private First Class Leonard relentlessly advanced, ultimately knocking out a second machinegun nest and capturing the roadblock objective. Private First Class Leonard's extraordinary heroism and selflessness above and beyond the call of duty are in keeping with the highest traditions of military service and reflect great credit upon himself, his unit, and the United States Army.

Mendoza, Manuel V.*

Staff sergeant Mendoza's military records were reviewed under the FY2002 National Defense Authorization Act, P.L. 107-107, Section 552. P.L. 107-107 requested that the DOD review service records of certain Jewish Americans or Hispanic Americans who had been awarded the Distinguished Service Cross, Navy Cross, or Air Force Cross.

Rank and organization: Staff Sergeant, Company B, 250th Infantry, 88th Infantry Division, U.S. Army. *Place and date:* Mount Battaglia, Italy, October 4, 1944. *Entered service at:* Phoenix, AZ. *Born:* June 15, 1922, Miami, AZ. *Date of issue:* March 18, 2014.

Citation: For conspicuous gallantry and intrepidity at the risk of his life above and beyond the call of duty:

Staff Sergeant Manuel V. Mendoza distinguished himself by acts of gallantry and intrepidity above and beyond the call of duty while serving as a platoon sergeant with Company B, 350th Infantry, 88th Infantry Division during combat operations against an armed enemy on Mount Battaglia, Italy, on October 4, 1944. That afternoon, the enemy launched a violent counterattack preceded by a heavy mortar barrage. Staff Sergeant Mendoza, already wounded in the arm and leg, grabbed a Thompson sub-machinegun and ran to the crest of the hill where he saw approximately 200 enemy troops charging up the slopes employing flame-throwers, machine pistols, rifles, and hand grenades. Staff Sergeant Mendoza immediately began to engage the enemy, firing five clips and killing 10 enemy soldiers. After exhausting his ammunition, he picked up a carbine and emptied its magazine at the enemy. By this time, an enemy soldier with a flame-thrower had almost reached the crest, but was quickly eliminated as Staff Sergeant

Mendoza drew his pistol and fired. Seeing that the enemy force continued to advance, Staff Sergeant Mendoza jumped into a machinegun emplacement that had just been abandoned and opened fire. Unable to engage the entire enemy force from his location, he picked up the machinegun and moved forward, firing from his hip and spraying a withering hail of bullets into the oncoming enemy, causing them to break into confusion. He then set the machinegun on the ground and continued to fire until the gun jammed. Without hesitating, Staff Sergeant Mendoza began throwing hand grenades at the enemy, causing them to flee. After the enemy had withdrawn, he advanced down the forward slope of the hill, retrieved numerous enemy weapons scattered about the area, captured a wounded enemy soldier, and returned to consolidate friendly positions with all available men. Staff Sergeant Mendoza's gallant stand resulted in 30 German soldiers killed and the successful defense of the hill. Staff Sergeant Mendoza's extraordinary heroism and selflessness above and beyond the call of duty are in keeping with the highest traditions of military service and reflect great credit upon himself, his unit, and the United States Army.

Moto, Kaoru*

Private Moto's military records were among those reviewed under the FY1996 National Defense Authorization Act (P.L. 104-106, Section 524). Following review, he was awarded the MOH.

Rank and organization: Private First Class, U.S. Army, Company C, 100th Infantry Battalion (Separate), 34th Infantry Division. *Place and date:* Near Castelina, Italy, July 7, 1944. *Entered service at:* Honolulu, HI, July 7, 1944. *Born:* unknown. *Date of issue:* June 21, 2000.

Citation: For conspicuous gallantry and intrepidity at the risk of his life above and beyond the call of duty:

Private First Class Kaoru Moto distinguished himself by extraordinary heroism in action on July 7, 1944, near Castellina, Italy. While serving as first scout, Private First Class Moto observed a machine gun nest that was hindering his platoon's progress. On his own initiative, he made his way to a point 10 paces from the hostile position and killed the enemy machinegunner. Immediately, the enemy assistant gunner opened fire in the direction of Private First Class Moto. Crawling to the rear of the position, Private First Class Moto surprised the enemy soldier, who quickly surrendered. Taking his prisoner with him, Private First Class Moto took a position a few yards from a house to prevent the enemy from using the building as an observation post. While guarding the house and his prisoner, he observed an enemy machine gun team moving into position. He engaged them and with deadly fire forced the enemy to withdraw. An enemy sniper located in another house fired at Private First Class Moto, severely wounding him. Applying first aid to his wound, he changed position to elude the sniper fire and to advance. Finally relieved of his position, he made his way to the rear for treatment. Crossing a road, he spotted an enemy machine gun nest. Opening fire, he wounded two of the three soldiers occupying the position. Not satisfied with this accomplishment, he then crawled forward to a better position and ordered the enemy soldier to surrender. Receiving no answer, Private First Class Moto fired at the position, and the soldiers surrendered.

Private First Class Moto's extraordinary heroism and devotion to duty are in keeping with the highest traditions of military service and reflect great credit on him, his unit, and the United States Army.

Muranaga, Kiyoshi K.*

Private Muranaga's military records were among those reviewed under the FY1996 National Defense Authorization Act (P.L. 104-106, Section 524). Following review, he was awarded the MOH.

Rank and organization: Private First Class, U.S. Army, Company F, 442nd Infantry Regiment, 34th Infantry Division. *Place and date:* Near Suvereto, Italy, June 26, 1944. *Entered service:* May 29, 1943. *Born:* February 16, 1922. *Date of issue:* June 21, 2000.

Citation: For conspicuous gallantry and intrepidity at the risk of his life above and beyond the call of duty:

Private First Class Kiyoshi K. Muranaga distinguished himself by extraordinary heroism in action on June 26,1944, near Suvereto, Italy. Private First Class Muranaga's company encountered a strong enemy force in commanding positions and with superior firepower. An enemy 88mm self-propelled gun opened direct fire on the company, causing the men to disperse and seek cover. Private First Class Muranaga's mortar squad was ordered to action, but the terrain made it impossible to set up their weapons. The squad leader, realizing the vulnerability of the mortar position, moved his men away from the gun to positions of relative safety. Because of the heavy casualties being inflicted on his company, Private First Class Muranaga, who served as a gunner, attempted to neutralize the 88mm weapon alone. Voluntarily remaining at his gun position, Private First Class Muranaga manned the mortar himself and opened fire on the enemy gun at a range of approximately 400 yards. With his third round, he was able to correct his fire so that the shell landed directly in front of the enemy gun. Meanwhile, the enemy crew, immediately aware of the source of mortar fire, turned their 88mm weapon directly on Private First Class Muranaga's position. Before Private First Class Muranaga could fire a fourth round, an 88mm shell scored a direct hit on his position, killing him instantly. Because of the accuracy of Private First Class Muranaga's previous fire, the enemy soldiers decided not to risk further exposure and immediately abandoned their position.

Private First Class Muranaga's extraordinary heroism and devotion to duty are in keeping with the highest traditions of military service and reflect great credit on him, his unit, and the United States Army.

Nakae, Masato*

Private Nakae's military records were among those reviewed under the FY1996 National Defense Authorization Act (P.L. 104-106, Section 524). Following review, he was awarded the MOH.

Rank and organization: Private, U.S. Army, Company A, 100th Battalion, 442nd Infantry Regiment. *Place and date:* Near Pisa, Italy, August 19, 1944. *Entered service at:* Honolulu, HI, February 8, 1942. *Born:* unknown. *Date of issue:* June 21, 2000.

Citation: For conspicuous gallantry and intrepidity at the risk of his life above and beyond the call of duty:

Private Masato Nakae distinguished himself by extraordinary heroism in action on 19 August 1944, near Pisa, Italy. When his submachine gun was damaged by a shell fragment during a fierce attack by a superior enemy force, Private Nakae quickly picked up his wounded comrade's M-1 rifle and fired rifle grenades at the steadily advancing enemy. As the hostile force continued to close in on his position, Private Nakae threw six grenades and forced them to withdraw. During a concentrated enemy mortar barrage that preceded the next assault by the enemy force, a mortar shell fragment seriously wounded Private Nakae. Despite his injury, he refused to surrender his position and continued firing at the advancing enemy. By inflicting heavy casualties on the enemy force, he finally succeeded in breaking up the attack and caused the enemy to withdraw.

Private Nakae's extraordinary heroism and devotion to duty are in keeping with the highest traditions of military service and reflect great credit on him, his unit, and the United States Army.

Nakamine, Shinyei*

Private Nakamine's military records were among those reviewed under the FY1996 National Defense Authorization Act (P.L. 104-106, Section 524). Following review, he was awarded the MOH.

Rank and organization: Private, U.S. Army, Company B, 100th Infantry Battalion (Separate), 34th Infantry Division. *Place and date:* Near La Torreto, Italy, June 2, 1944. *Entered service at:* Honolulu, HI, November 14, 1941. *Born:* February 26, 1920. *Date of issue:* June 21, 2000.

Citation: For conspicuous gallantry and intrepidity at the risk of his life above and beyond the call of duty.

Private Shinyei Nakamine distinguished himself by extraordinary heroism in action on 2 June 1944, near La Torreto, Italy. During an attack, Private Nakamine's platoon became pinned down by intense machine gun crossfire from a small knoll 200 yards to the front. On his own initiative, Private Nakamine crawled toward one of the hostile weapons. Reaching a point 25 yards from the enemy, he charged the machine gun nest, firing his submachine gun, and killed three enemy soldiers and captured two. Later that afternoon, Private Nakamine discovered an enemy soldier on the right flank of his platoon's position. Crawling 25 yards from his position, Private Nakamine opened fire and killed the soldier. Then, seeing a machine gun nest to his front approximately 75 yards away, he returned to his platoon and led an automatic rifle team toward the enemy. Under covering fire from his team, Private Nakamine crawled to a point 25 yards from the nest and threw hand grenades at the enemy soldiers, wounding one and capturing four. Spotting another machine gun nest 100 yards to his right flank, he led the automatic rifle team toward the hostile position but was killed by a burst of machine gun fire.

Private Nakamine's extraordinary heroism and devotion to duty are in keeping with the highest traditions of military service and reflect great credit on him, his unit, and the United States Army.

Nakamura, William K.*

Private Nakamura's military records were among those reviewed under the FY1996 National Defense Authorization Act (P.L. 104-106, Section 524). Following review, he was awarded the MOH.

Rank and organization: Private First Class, U.S. Army, Company G, 442nd Regiment, 34th Infantry Division. *Place and date:* Near Castellina, Italy, July 4, 1944. *Entered service:* July 27, 1943. *Born:* January 21, 1922. *Date of issue:* June 21, 2000.

Citation: For conspicuous gallantry and intrepidity at the risk of his life above and beyond the call of duty.

Private First Class William K. Nakamura distinguished himself by extraordinary heroism in action on 4 July 1944, near Castellina, Italy. During a fierce firefight, Private First Class Nakamura's platoon became pinned down by enemy machine gun fire from a concealed position. On his own initiative, Private First Class Nakamura crawled 20 yards toward the hostile nest, with fire from the enemy machine gun barely missing him. Reaching a point 15 yards from the position, he quickly raised himself to a kneeling position and threw four hand grenades, killing or wounding at least three of the enemy soldiers. The enemy weapon silenced, Private First Class Nakamura crawled back to his platoon, which was able to continue its advance as a result of his courageous action. Later, his company was ordered to withdraw from the crest of a hill so that a mortar barrage could be placed on the ridge. On his own initiative, Private First Class Nakamura remained in position to cover his comrades' withdrawal. While moving toward the safety of a wooded draw, his platoon became pinned down by deadly machine gun fire. Crawling to a point from which he could fire on the enemy position, Private First Class Nakamura quickly and accurately fired his weapon to pin down the enemy machine gunners. His platoon was then able to withdraw to safety without further casualties. Private First Class Nakamura was killed during this heroic stand.

Private First Class Nakamura's extraordinary heroism and devotion to duty are in keeping with the highest traditions of military service and reflect great credit on him, his unit, and the United States Army.

Nietzel, Alfred B.*

Rank and organization: Sergeant, Company H, 16th Infantry Regiment, 1st Infantry Division, U.S. Army. *Place and date:* Heistern, Germany, November 18, 1944. *Entered service at:* Jamaica, NY. *Born:* April 27, 1921, Queens, NY. *Date of issue:* March 18, 2014.

Citation: For conspicuous gallantry and intrepidity at the risk of his life above and beyond the call of duty:

Sergeant Alfred B. Nietzel distinguished himself by acts of gallantry and intrepidity above and beyond the call of duty while serving as a section leader for Company H, 16th Infantry Regiment, 1st Infantry Division during combat operations against an armed enemy in Heistern, Germany, on November 18, 1944. That afternoon, Sergeant Nietzel fought tenaciously to repel a vicious enemy attack against his unit. Sergeant Nietzel employed accurate, intense fire from his machinegun and successfully slowed the hostile advance. However, the overwhelming enemy force continued to press forward. Realizing he desperately needed reinforcements, Sergeant Nietzel ordered the three remaining members of his squad to return to the company command post and secure aid. He immediately turned his attention to covering their movement with his fire. After expending all his machinegun ammunition, Sergeant Nietzel began firing his rifle into the attacking ranks until he was killed by the explosion of an enemy grenade. Sergeant Nietzel's extraordinary heroism and selflessness at the cost of his own life, above and beyond the call of duty, are in keeping with the highest traditions of military service and reflect great credit upon himself, his unit, and the United States Army.

Nishimoto, Joe M.*

Private Nishimoto's military records were among those reviewed under the FY1996 National Defense Authorization Act (P.L. 104-106, Section 524). Following review, he was awarded the MOH.

Rank and organization: Private, First Class, U.S. Army, Company G, 442nd Regimental Combat Team (Attached to the Third Battalion). *Place and date:* Vicinity of La Houssiere, France, November 7, 1944. *Entered service:* unknown. *Born:* circa 1920. *Date of issue:* June 21, 2000.

Citation: For conspicuous gallantry and intrepidity at the risk of his life above and beyond the call of duty.

Private First Class Joe M. Nishimoto distinguished himself by extraordinary heroism in action on 7 November 1944, near La Houssiere, France. After three days of unsuccessful attempts by his company to dislodge the enemy from a strongly defended ridge, Private First Class Nishimoto, as acting squad leader, boldly crawled forward through a heavily mined and booby-trapped area. Spotting a machine gun nest, he hurled a grenade and destroyed the emplacement. Then, circling to the rear of another machine gun position, he fired his submachine gun at point-blank range, killing one gunner and wounding another. Pursuing two enemy riflemen, Private First Class Nishimoto killed one, while the other hastily retreated. Continuing his determined assault, he drove another machine gun crew from its position. The enemy, with their key strong points taken, were forced to withdraw from this sector.

Private First Class Nishimoto's extraordinary heroism and devotion to duty are in keeping with the highest traditions of military service and reflect great credit on him, his unit, and the United States Army.

Ohata, Allan M.*

Sergeant Ohata's military records were among those reviewed under the FY1996 National Defense Authorization Act (P.L. 104-106, Section 524). Following review, he was awarded the MOH.

Rank and organization: Staff Sergeant, U.S. Army, Company B, 100th Infantry Battalion (Separate), 34th Infantry Division. *Place and date:* Near Cerasuolo, November 29-30, 1943. *Entered service at:* Honolulu, HI, November 21, 1941. *Born:* September 13, 1918, Honolulu, HI. *Date of issue:* June 21, 2000.

Citation: For conspicuous gallantry and intrepidity at the risk of his life above and beyond the call of duty.

Sergeant Allan M. Ohata distinguished himself by extraordinary heroism in action on November 29 and 30, 1943, near Cerasuolo, Italy. Sergeant Ohata, his squad leader, and three men were ordered to protect his platoon's left flank against an attacking enemy force of 40 men, armed with machine guns, machine pistols, and rifles. He posted one of his men, an automatic rifleman, on the extreme left, 15 yards from his own position. Taking his position, Sergeant Ohata delivered effective fire against the advancing enemy. The man to his left called for assistance when his automatic rifle was shot and damaged. With utter disregard for his personal safety, Sergeant Ohata left his position and advanced 15 yards through heavy machine gun fire. Reaching his comrade's position, he immediately fired upon the enemy, killing 10 enemy soldiers and successfully covering his comrade's withdrawal to replace his damaged weapon. Sergeant Ohata and the automatic rifleman held their position and killed 37 enemy soldiers. Both men then charged the three remaining soldiers and captured them. Later, Sergeant Ohata and the automatic rifleman stopped another attacking force of 14, killing four and wounding three while the others fled. The following day, he and the automatic rifleman held their flank with grim determination and staved off all attacks.

Staff Sergeant Ohata's extraordinary heroism and devotion to duty are in keeping with the highest traditions of military service and reflect great credit on him, his unit, and the United States Army.

Okubo, James K.

Congress approved "a bill to authorize the award of the Medal of Honor" to Technician Okubo and others on June 20, 2000, removing the statutory time limit on the award.

Rank and organization: Technician Fifth Grade, Medical Corps, U.S. Army, Medical Detachment, 442nd Combat Team. *Place and date:* Near Biffontaine, France, October 28 and 29, 1944 and

November 4, 1944. *Entered service at:* Alturas, CA, May 22, 1943. *Born:* Anacortes, WA. *Date of issue:* June 21, 2000.

Citation: For conspicuous gallantry and intrepidity at the risk of his life above and beyond the call of duty.

Technician Fifth Grade James K. Okubo distinguished himself by extraordinary heroism in action on October 28 and 29, 1944, and November 4, 1944, in the Forêt Domaniale de Champ, near Biffontaine, eastern France. On October 28, under strong enemy fire coming from behind mine fields and roadblocks, Technician Fifth Grade Okubo, a medic, crawled 150 yards to within 40 yards of the enemy lines. Two grenades were thrown at him while he left his last covered position to carry back wounded comrades. Under constant barrages of enemy small arms and machine gun fire, he treated 17 men on October 28, and 8 more men on October 29. On November 4, Technician Fifth Grade Okubo ran 75 yards under grazing machine gun fire and, while exposed to hostile fire directed at him, evacuated and treated a seriously wounded crewman from a burning tank, who otherwise would have died.

Technician Fifth Grade James K. Okubo's extraordinary heroism and devotion to duty are in keeping with the highest traditions of military service and reflect great credit on him, his unit, and the United States Army.

Okutsu, Yukio

Sergeant Okutsu's military records were among those reviewed under the FY1996 National Defense Authorization Act (P.L. 104-106, Section 524). Following review, he was awarded the MOH.

Rank and organization: Technical Sergeant, U.S. Army, Company F, 442nd Regimental Combat Team. *Place and date:* On Mount Belvedere near Massa, Italy, April 7, 1945. *Entered service at:* Hanapepe, HI, March 12, 1943. *Born:* November 3, 1921, Koloa, HI. *Date of issue:* June 21, 2000.

Citation: For conspicuous gallantry and intrepidity at the risk of his life above and beyond the call of duty.

Technical Sergeant Yukio Okutsu distinguished himself by extraordinary heroism in action on April 7, 1945, on Mount Belvedere, Italy. While his platoon was halted by the crossfire of three machine guns, Technical Sergeant Okutsu boldly crawled to within 30 yards of the nearest enemy emplacement through heavy fire. He destroyed the position with two accurately placed hand grenades, killing three machine gunners. Crawling and dashing from cover to cover, he threw another grenade, silencing a second machine gun, wounding two enemy soldiers, and forcing two others to surrender. Seeing a third machine gun, which obstructed his platoon's advance, he moved forward through heavy small arms fire and was stunned momentarily by rifle fire, which glanced off his helmet. Recovering, he bravely charged several enemy riflemen with his submachine gun, forcing them to withdraw from their positions. Then, rushing the machine gun nest, he captured the weapon and its entire crew of four. By these single-handed actions he enabled his platoon to resume its assault on a vital objective. The courageous performance of Technical Sergeant Okutsu against formidable odds was an inspiration to all.

Technical Sergeant Okutsu's extraordinary heroism and devotion to duty are in keeping with the highest traditions of military service and reflect great credit on him, his unit, and the United States Army.

Ono, Frank H.*

Private Ono's military records were among those reviewed under the FY1996 National Defense Authorization Act (P.L. 104-106, Section 524). Following review, he was awarded the Medal of Honor.

Rank and organization: Private, U.S. Army, Company G, 442nd Regimental Combat Team. *Place and date:* Near Castellina, Italy. *Entered service at:* Knox, Indiana, September 2, 1943. *Born:* June 6, 1923. *Date of issue:* June 21, 2000.

Citation: For conspicuous gallantry and intrepidity at the risk of his life above and beyond the call of duty.

Private First Class Frank H. Ono distinguished himself by extraordinary heroism in action on July 4, 1944, near Castellina, Italy. In attacking a heavily defended hill, Private First Class Ono's squad was caught in a hail of formidable fire from the well-entrenched enemy. Private First Class Ono opened fire with his automatic rifle and silenced one machine gun 300 hundred yards to the right front. Advancing through incessant fire, he killed a sniper with another burst of fire, and while his squad leader reorganized the rest of the platoon in the rear, he alone defended the critical position. His weapon was then wrenched from his grasp by a burst of enemy machine pistol fire as enemy troops attempted to close in on him. Hurling hand grenades, Private First Class Ono forced the enemy to abandon the attempt, resolutely defending the newly won ground until the rest of the platoon moved forward. Taking a wounded comrade's rifle, Private First Class Ono again joined in the assault. After killing two more enemy soldiers, he boldly ran through withering automatic, small arms, and mortar fire to render first aid to his platoon leader and a seriously wounded rifleman. In danger of being encircled, the platoon was ordered to withdraw. Volunteering to cover the platoon, Private First Class Ono occupied virtually unprotected positions near the crest of the hill, engaging an enemy machine gun emplaced on an adjoining ridge and exchanging fire with snipers armed with machine pistols. Completely disregarding his own safety, he made himself the constant target of concentrated enemy fire until the platoon reached the comparative safety of a draw. He then descended the hill in stages, firing his rifle, until he rejoined the platoon.

Private First Class Ono's extraordinary heroism and devotion to duty are in keeping with the highest traditions of military service and reflect great credit on him, his unit, and the United States Army.

Otani, Kazuo*

Sergeant Otani's military records were among those reviewed under the FY1996 National Defense Authorization Act (P.L. 104-106, Section 524). Following review, he was awarded the Medal of Honor.

Rank and organization: Staff Sergeant, U.S. Army, Company G, 442nd Infantry Regiment, 34th Infantry Division. *Place and date:* Near Pieve di S. Luce, Italy, July 15, 1944. *Entered service at:* Indianapolis, IN, February 16, 1942. *Born:* June 2, 1918. *Date of issue:* June 21, 2000.

Citation: For conspicuous gallantry and intrepidity at the risk of his life above and beyond the call of duty.

Staff Sergeant Kazuo Otani distinguished himself by extraordinary heroism in action on July 15, 1944, near Pieve Di S. Luce, Italy. Advancing to attack a hill objective, Staff Sergeant Otani's platoon became pinned down in a wheat field by concentrated fire from enemy machine gun and sniper positions. Realizing the danger confronting his platoon, Staff Sergeant Otani left his cover and shot and killed a sniper who was firing with deadly effect upon the platoon. Followed by a steady stream of machine gun bullets, Staff Sergeant Otani then dashed across the open wheat field toward the foot of a cliff, and directed his men to crawl to the cover of the cliff. When the movement of the platoon drew heavy enemy fire, he dashed along the cliff toward the left flank, exposing himself to enemy fire. By attracting the attention of the enemy, he enabled the men closest to the cliff to reach cover. Organizing these men to guard against possible enemy counterattack, Staff Sergeant Otani again made his way across the open field, shouting instructions to the stranded men while continuing to draw enemy fire. Reaching the rear of the platoon position, he took partial cover in a shallow ditch and directed covering fire for the men who had begun to move forward. At this point, one of his men became seriously wounded. Ordering his men to remain under cover, Staff Sergeant Otani crawled to the wounded soldier, who was lying on open ground in full view of the enemy. Dragging the wounded soldier to a shallow ditch, Staff Sergeant Otani proceeded to render first aid treatment, but was mortally wounded by machine gun fire.

Staff Sergeant Otani's extraordinary heroism and devotion to duty are in keeping with the highest traditions of military service and reflect great credit on him, his unit, and the United States Army.

Rivers, Ruben*

Sergeant Rivers was among the seven African Americans who were awarded the MOH for their heroic acts during World War II following Congress's approval of P.L. 104-201, which waived the time limit to allow the President to award the MOH.

Rank and organization: Staff Sergeant, U.S. Army, Company A, 761ˢᵗ Tank Battalion. *Place and date:* Near Guebling, France, November 16-19, 1944. *Entered service:* January 15, 1942. *Born:* October 30, 1918, Oklahoma City, OK. *Date of issue:* January 13, 1997.

Citation: Staff Sergeant Ruben Rivers distinguished himself by extraordinary heroism in action during November 15-19, 1944, while serving with Company A, 761ˢᵗ Tank Battalion.

On November 16, 1944, while advancing toward the town of Guebling, France, Staff Sergeant Rivers' tank hit a mine at a railroad crossing. Although severely wounded, his leg slashed to the bone, Staff Sergeant Rivers declined an injection of morphine, refused to be evacuated, took command of another tank, and advanced with his company into Guebling the next day. Repeatedly refusing evacuation, Staff Sergeant Rivers continued to direct his tank's fire at enemy positions beyond the town through the morning of November 19, 1944. At dawn that day, Company A's tanks advanced toward Bourgaltroff, their next objective, but were stopped by enemy fire. Captain David J. Williams, the company commander, ordered his tanks to withdraw and take cover. Staff Sergeant Rivers, however radioed that he had spotted the German antitank positions: "I see 'em. We'll fight 'em!" Staff Sergeant Rivers, joined by another Company A tank, opened fire on enemy tanks, covering Company A as they withdrew. While doing so, Staff Sergeant Rivers's tank was hit, killing him and wounding the rest of the crew.

Staff Sergeant Rivers's fighting spirit and daring leadership were an inspiration to his unit and exemplify the highest traditions of military service.

Sakato, George T.

Private Sakato's military records were among those reviewed under the FY1996 National Defense Authorization Act (P.L. 104-106, Section 524). Following review, he was awarded the MOH.

Rank and organization: Private, U.S. Army, Company E, 442nd Regimental Combat Team. *Place and date:* Near Biffontaine, France, October 29,1944. *Entered service at:* Fort Douglas, UT, March 1, 1944. *Born:* February 19, 1921, Colton, CA. *Date of issue:* June 21, 2000.

Citation: For conspicuous gallantry and intrepidity at the risk of his life above and beyond the call of duty.

Private George T. Sakato distinguished himself by extraordinary heroism in action on 29 October 1944, on hill 617 in the vicinity of Biffontaine, France. After his platoon had virtually destroyed two enemy defense lines, during which he personally killed five enemy soldiers and captured four, his unit was pinned down by heavy enemy fire. Disregarding the enemy fire, Private Sakato made a one-man rush that encouraged his platoon to charge and destroy the enemy strongpoint. While his platoon was reorganizing, he proved to be the inspiration of his squad in halting a counter-attack on the left flank during which his squad leader was killed. Taking charge of the squad, he continued his relentless tactics, using an enemy rifle and P-38 pistol to stop an organized enemy attack. During this entire action, he killed 12 and wounded two, personally captured four, and assisted his platoon in taking 34 prisoners. By continuously ignoring enemy fire, and by his gallant courage and fighting spirit, he turned impending defeat into victory and helped his platoon complete its mission.

Private Sakato's extraordinary heroism and devotion to duty are in keeping with the highest traditions of military service and reflect great credit on him, his unit, and the United States Army.

Salomon, Ben L.*

Congress approved the FY2002 National Defense Authorization Act, P.L. 107-107, Section 551, on December 28, 2001, removing the statutory time limit on the award for Captain Salomon.

Rank and organization: Captain, U.S. Army 2nd Battalion, 105th Infantry Regiment, 27th Infantry Division. *Place and date:* Saipan, Marianas Islands, July 7, 1944. *Entered service:* Denver, CO. *Born:* September 1, 1914, Milwaukee, WI. *Date of issue:* May 1, 2002.

Citation: For conspicuous gallantry and intrepidity at the risk of his life above and beyond the call of duty.

Captain Ben L. Salomon was serving at Saipan, in the Marianas Islands on July 7, 1944, as the Surgeon for the 2d Battalion, 105th Infantry Regiment, 27th Infantry Division. The Regiment's 1st and 2d Battalions were attacked by an overwhelming force estimated between 3,000 and 5,000 Japanese soldiers. It was one of the largest attacks attempted in the Pacific Theater during World War II. Although both units fought furiously, the enemy soon penetrated the Battalions' combined perimeter and inflicted overwhelming casualties. In the first minutes of the attack, approximately 30 wounded soldiers walked, crawled, or were carried into Captain Salomon's aid station, and the small tent soon filled with wounded men. As the perimeter began to be overrun, it became increasingly difficult for Captain Salomon to work on the wounded. He then saw a Japanese soldier bayoneting one of the wounded soldiers lying near the tent. Firing from a squatting position, Captain Salomon quickly killed the enemy soldier. Then, as he turned his attention back to the wounded, two more Japanese soldiers appeared in the front entrance of the tent. As these enemy soldiers were killed, four more crawled under the tent walls. Rushing them, Captain Salomon kicked the knife out of the hand of one, shot another, and bayoneted a third. Captain Salomon butted the fourth enemy soldier in the stomach and a wounded comrade then shot and killed the enemy soldier. Realizing the gravity of the situation, Captain Salomon ordered the wounded to make their way as best they could back to the regimental aid station, while he attempted to hold off the enemy until they were clear. Captain Salomon then grabbed a rifle from one of the wounded and rushed out of the tent. After four men were killed while manning a machine gun, Captain Salomon took control of it. When his body was later found, 98 dead enemy soldiers were piled in front of his position.

Captain Salomon's extraordinary heroism and devotion to duty are in keeping with the highest traditions of military service and reflect great credit upon himself, his unit, and the United States Army.

Schwab, Donald K.*

Congress approved the FY2002 National Defense Authorization Act, P.L. 107-107, Section 552, on December 28, 2001, requesting that the DOD review service records of certain Jewish Americans or Hispanic Americans who had been awarded the Distinguished Service Cross, Navy Cross, or Air Force Cross.

Rank and organization: First Lieutenant, Company E, 15th Infantry Regiment, 3d Infantry Division, U.S. Army. *Place and date:* Lure, France, September 17, 1944. *Born:* December 6, 1918, Hooper, NE. *Date of issue:* March 18, 2014.

Citation: For conspicuous gallantry and intrepidity at the risk of his life above and beyond the call of duty:

First Lieutenant Donald K. Schwab distinguished himself by acts of gallantry and intrepidity above and beyond the call of duty while serving as the commander of Company E, 15th Infantry Regiment, 3rd Infantry Division, during combat operations against an armed enemy near Lure, France, on September 17, 1944. That afternoon, as First Lieutenant Schwab led his company across four hundred yards of exposed ground, an intense, grazing burst of machinegun and machine-pistol fire sprung forth without warning from a fringe of woods directly in front of the American force. First Lieutenant Schwab quickly extricated his men from the attempted ambush and led them back to a defiladed position. Soon after, he was ordered to overwhelm the enemy line. He rapidly organized his men into a skirmish line and, with indomitable courage, again led them forward into the lethal enemy fire. When halted a second time, First Lieutenant Schwab moved from man to man to supervise collection of the wounded and organize his company's withdrawal. From defilade, he rallied his decimated force for a third charge on the hostile strong point and successfully worked his way to within fifty yards of the Germans before ordering his men to hit the dirt. While automatic weapons fire blazed around him, he rushed forward alone, firing his carbine at the German foxholes, aiming for the vital enemy machine-pistol nest that had sparked the German resistance and caused heavy casualties among his men. Silhouetted through the mist and rain by enemy flares, he charged to the German emplacement, ripped the half-cover off the hostile firing pit, struck the German gunner on the head with his carbine butt, and dragged the German back through a hail of fire to friendly lines. First Lieutenant Schwab's action so disorganized hostile infantry resistance that the enemy forces withdrew, abandoning their formidable defensive line. First Lieutenant Schwab's extraordinary heroism and selflessness above and beyond the call of duty are in keeping with the highest traditions of military service and reflect great credit upon himself, his unit, and the United States Army.

Tanouye, Ted T.*

Sergeant Tanouye's military records were among those reviewed under the FY1996 National Defense Authorization Act (P.L. 104-106, Section 524). Following review, he was awarded the MOH.

Rank and organization: Technical Sergeant, U.S. Army, Company K, 442nd Infantry Regiment, 34th Infantry Division. *Place and date:* Near Molino A Ventoabbto, Italy, July 7, 1944. *Entered service:* February 21, 1942. *Born:* November 14, 1919. *Date of issue:* June 21, 2000.

Citation: For conspicuous gallantry and intrepidity at the risk of his life above and beyond the call of duty.

Technical Sergeant Ted T. Tanouye distinguished himself by extraordinary heroism in action on 7 July 1944, near Molino A Ventoabbto, Italy. Technical Sergeant Tanouye led his platoon in an attack to capture the crest of a strategically important hill that afforded little cover. Observing an enemy machine gun crew placing its gun in position to his left front, Technical Sergeant Tanouye crept forward a few yards and opened fire on the position, killing or wounding three and causing two others to disperse. Immediately, an enemy machine pistol opened fire on him. He returned the fire and killed or wounded three more enemy soldiers. While advancing forward, Technical Sergeant Tanouye was subjected to grenade bursts, which severely wounded his left arm. Sighting an enemy-held trench, he raked the position with fire from his submachine gun and wounded several of the enemy. Running out of ammunition, he crawled 20 yards to obtain several clips from a comrade on his left flank. Next, sighting an enemy machine pistol that had pinned down his men, Technical Sergeant Tanouye crawled forward a few yards and threw a hand grenade into the position, silencing the pistol. He then located another enemy machine gun firing down the slope of the hill, opened fire on it, and silenced that position. Drawing fire from a machine pistol nest located above him, he opened fire on it and wounded three of its occupants. Finally taking his objective, Technical Sergeant Tanouye organized a defensive position on the reverse slope of the hill before accepting first aid treatment and evacuation.

Technical Sergeant Tanouye's extraordinary heroism and devotion to duty are in keeping with the highest traditions of military service and reflect great credit on him, his unit, and the United States Army.

Thomas, Charles L.*

Lieutenant Thomas was among the seven African Americans who were awarded the MOH for their heroic acts during World War II following Congress's approval of P.L. 104-201, which waived the time limit to allow the President to award the MOH.

Rank and organization: Lieutenant, Company C, 614th Tank Destroyer Battalion, U.S. Army. *Place and date:* Near Climbach, France, December 14, 1944. *Entered service:* January 20, 1942. *Born:* April 17,1920, Birmingham, AL. *Date of issue:* January 13, 1997.

Citation: Then Lieutenant Charles L. Thomas distinguished himself by extraordinary heroism in action on December 14, 1944. One platoon of Company C, 614th Tank Destroyer Battalion, was designated as the leading element in a task force formed to storm and capture the village of Climbach, France.

Lieutenant Thomas, the commanding officer of Company C, realized, with the obscurity of information regarding the enemy and a complete lack of reconnaissance, the mission would be an extremely dangerous one. Fully cognizant of the danger, Lieutenant Thomas volunteered to command the selected platoon of his company and ride in the column's leading vehicle—a highly maneuverable, but equally vulnerable, M-20 scout car. Lieutenant Thomas knew that if there was a concentration of enemy armor in the village, as was believed, he would absorb the initial shock of the first enemy resistance. The task force left Preuschdorf, France, at 1023 hours, and proceeded to advance in column toward Climbach. Lieutenant Thomas in his scout car stayed well in form of the column. At 1400 hours, upon reaching the high ground southeast of the village, Lieutenant Thomas experienced initial contact with the enemy. As his scout car advanced to an exposed position on the heights, he received intense direct fire from enemy artillery, self-propelled guns, and small arms at a range of 700 yards. The first burst of hostile fire disabled the scout car and severely wounded Lieutenant Thomas. He immediately signaled the column to halt. Before leaving the wrecked vehicle, Lieutenant Thomas and the crew found themselves subjected to a veritable hail of enemy fire. Lieutenant Thomas received multiple gunshot wounds in his chest, legs, and left arm. In spite of the intense pain caused by his wounds, Lieutenant Thomas ordered and directed the dispersion and emplacement of his first two antitank guns. In a few minutes these guns were effectively returning the enemy fire. Realizing that it would be impossible for him to remain in command of the platoon because of his injuries, Lieutenant Thomas then signaled for the platoon commander to join him. Lieutenant Thomas then thoroughly oriented him as to the enemy gun positions, his ammunition status, and the general situation. Although fully cognizant of the probable drastic consequences of not receiving prompt medical attention, Lieutenant Thomas refused evacuation until he felt certain that his junior officer was in full control of the situation. Only then did Lieutenant Thomas allow his evacuation to the rear. Throughout the action, Lieutenant Thomas displayed magnificent personal courage and a complete disregard for his own safety. His extraordinary heroism spurred the soldiers of the platoon to a fierce determination to triumph, and resulted in a mass display of heroism by them.

Lieutenant Thomas's intrepid actions throughout the operation reflect the highest traditions of military service.

Urban, Matt

Lieutenant Urban's recommendation was delayed due to administrative error. The law provides that in such cases time limitations may be waived.[11]

Rank and organization: Lieutenant Colonel, Second Battalion, 60th Infantry Regiment, Ninth Infantry Division, U.S. Army. *Place and date:* Renouf, St. Lo, France, the Meuse River near Heer, Belgium, June 14,1944, to September 3, 1944. *Entered service at:* Fort Bragg, NC, July 2, 1941. *Born:* August 25, 1919, Buffalo, NY. *Date of issue:* July 19, 1980.[12]

Citation: For conspicuous gallantry and intrepidity in action at the risk of life above and beyond the call of duty:

During the period, June 14, 1944, to September 3, 1944, Lieutenant Colonel (then Captain) Matt Urban distinguished himself by a series of bold, heroic actions, exemplified by singularly outstanding combat leadership, personal bravery, and tenacious devotion to duty, while assigned to the Second Battalion, 60th Infantry Regiment, Ninth Infantry Division. On 14 June, Captain Urban's company, attacking at Renouf, France, encountered heavy enemy small arms and tank fire. The enemy tanks were unmercifully raking his unit's positions and inflicting heavy casualties. Captain Urban, realizing that his company was in imminent danger of being decimated, armed himself with a bazooka. He worked his way with an ammo carrier through hedgerows, under a continuing barrage of fire, to a point near the tanks. He brazenly exposed himself to the enemy fire and, firing the bazooka, destroyed both tanks. Responding to Captain Urban's action, his company moved forward and routed the enemy. Later that same day, still in the attack near Orglandes, Captain Urban was wounded in the leg by direct fire from a 37mm tank-gun. He refused evacuation and continued to lead his company until they moved into

---

[11] 10 U.S.C. §3744, 6248, 8744.

[12] *Washington Post*, "35 years Late, Veteran Receives Medal of Honor," July 20, 1980.

defensive positions for the night. At 0500 hours the next day, still in the attack near Orglandes, Captain Urban, though badly wounded, directed his company in another attack. One hour later he was again wounded. Suffering from two wounds, one serious, he was evacuated to England. In mid-July, while recovering from his wounds, he learned of his unit's severe losses in the hedgerows of Normandy. Realizing his unit's need for battle-tested leaders, he voluntarily left the hospital and hitchhiked his way back to his unit near St. Lo, France. Arriving at the Second Battalion Command Post at 1130 hours, 25 July, he found that his unit had jumped-off at 1100 hours in the first attack of "Operation Cobra." Still limping from his leg wound, Captain Urban made his way forward to retake command of his company. He found his company held up by strong enemy opposition. Two supporting tanks had been destroyed and another, intact but with no tank commander or gunner, was not moving. He located a lieutenant in charge of the support tanks and directed a plan of attack to eliminate the enemy strong-point. The lieutenant and a sergeant were immediately killed by the heavy enemy fire when they tried to mount the tank. Captain Urban, though physically hampered by his leg wound and knowing quick action had to be taken, dashed through the scathing fire and mounted the tank. With enemy bullets ricocheting from the tank, Captain Urban ordered the tank forward and, completely exposed to the enemy fire, manned the machine gun and placed devastating fire on the enemy. His action, in the face of enemy fire, galvanized the battalion into action, and they attacked and destroyed the enemy position. On 2 August, Captain Urban was wounded in the chest by shell fragments and, disregarding the recommendation of the Battalion Surgeon, again refused evacuation. On 6 August, Captain Urban became the commander of the Second Battalion. On 15 August, he was again wounded but remained with his unit. On 3 September, the Second Battalion was given the mission of establishing a crossing-point on the Meuse River near Heer, Belgium. The enemy planned to stop the advance of the allied Army by concentrating heavy forces at the Meuse. The Second Battalion, attacking toward the crossing-point, encountered fierce enemy artillery, small arms, and mortar fire, which stopped the attack. Captain Urban quickly moved from his command post to the lead position of the battalion. Reorganizing the attacking elements, he personally led a charge toward the enemy's strong-point. As the charge moved across the open terrain, Captain Urban was seriously wounded in the neck. Although unable to talk above a whisper from the paralyzing neck wound, and in danger of losing his life, he refused to be evacuated until the enemy was routed and his battalion had secured the crossing-point on the Meuse River.

Captain Urban's personal leadership, limitless bravery, and repeated extraordinary exposure to enemy fire served as an inspiration to his entire battalion. His valorous and intrepid actions reflect the utmost credit on him and uphold the noble traditions of the United States Army.

Wai, Francis B.*

Captain Wai's military records were among those reviewed under the FY1996 National Defense Authorization Act (P.L. 104-106, Section 524). Following review, he was awarded the MOH.

Rank and organization: Captain, U.S. Infantry Headquarters, 34th Infantry Regiment, U.S. Army. *Place and date:* Near Leyte, Philippine Islands, October 20, 1944. *Entered service:* unknown. *Born:* unknown. *Date of issue:* June 21, 2000.

Citation: For conspicuous gallantry and intrepidity at the risk of his life above and beyond the call of duty.

Captain Francis B. Wai distinguished himself by extraordinary heroism in action, on October 20, 1944, in Leyte, Philippine Islands. Captain Wai landed at Red Beach, Leyte, in the face of accurate, concentrated enemy fire from gun positions advantageously located in a palm grove bounded by submerged rice paddies. Finding the first four waves of American soldiers leaderless, disorganized, and pinned down on the open beach, he immediately assumed command. Issuing clear and concise orders, and disregarding heavy enemy machine gun and rifle fire, he began to move inland through the rice paddies without cover. The men, inspired by his cool demeanor and heroic example, rose from their positions and followed him. During the advance, Captain Wai repeatedly determined the locations of enemy strong points by deliberately exposing himself to draw their fire. In leading an assault upon the last remaining Japanese pillbox in the area, he was killed by its occupants. Captain Wai's courageous, aggressive leadership inspired the men, even after his death, to advance and destroy the enemy. His intrepid and determined efforts were largely responsible for the rapidity with which the initial beachhead was secured.

Captain Wai's extraordinary heroism and devotion to duty are in keeping with the highest traditions of military service and reflect great credit on him, his unit, and the United States Army.

Watson, George*

Private Watson was among the seven African Americans who were awarded the MOH for their heroic acts during World War II following Congress's approval of P.L. 104-201, which waived the time limit to allow the President to award the MOH.

Rank and organization: Private, Second Battalion, 29th Quartermaster Regiment, U.S. Army. *Place and date:* Near Porlock Harbor, New Guinea, 8 March 1943. *Entered service:* 1 September 1942. *Born:* 24 March 1914, Birmingham, AL. *Date of issue:* January 13, 1997.

Citation: Private George Watson distinguished himself by extraordinary heroism on 8 March 1943, while serving in the Pacific Command with the Second Battalion, 29th Quartermaster Regiment, near Porlock Harbor, New Guinea.

Private Watson was on board a troop ship, the Dutch Steamer (United States Army Transport) *Jacob*, when it was attacked and hit by enemy bombers. Before it sank, the ship was abandoned. Private Watson, instead of seeking to save himself, remained in deep waters long enough to assist several soldiers who could not swim to reach the safety of a life raft. This heroic action, which subsequently cost him his life, resulted in saving the lives of several of his comrades. Weakened by continuous physical exertion and overcome by muscular fatigue, Private Watson drowned when the suction of the sinking ship dragged him beneath the surface of the swirling waters. His demonstrated bravery and unselfish act set in motion a train of compelling events that finally led to American victory in the Pacific.

Private Watson's extraordinary valorous actions, his daring and inspiring leadership, and his self-sacrificing devotion to his fellow man exemplify the finest traditions of military service.

Korean War

Baldonado, Joe R.*

Corporal Baldonado's military records were reviewed under the FY2002 National Defense Authorization Act, in which Congress requested that the DOD review service records of certain Jewish Americans or Hispanic Americans who had been awarded the Distinguished Service Cross, Navy Cross, or Air Force Cross.

Rank and organization: Corporal, Company B, 187th Airborne Infantry Regiment, U.S. Army. *Place and date:* Kangdong, Korea, November 25, 1950. *Entered service at:* Santa Clara, CA. *Born:* August 28, 1930, Colorado. *Date of issue:* March 18, 2014.

Citation: For conspicuous gallantry and intrepidity at the risk of his life above and beyond the call of duty:

Corporal Joe R. Baldonado distinguished himself by acts of gallantry and intrepidity above and beyond the call of duty while serving as an acting machinegunner in 3rd Squad, 2nd Platoon, Company B, 187th Airborne Infantry Regiment during combat operations against an armed enemy in Kangdong, Korea, on November 25, 1950. On that morning, the enemy launched a strong attack in an effort to seize the hill occupied by Corporal Baldonado and his company. The platoon had expended most of its ammunition in repelling the enemy attack and the platoon leader decided to commit his 3rd Squad, with its supply of ammunition, in the defensive action. Since there was no time to dig in because of the proximity of the enemy, who had advanced to within 25 yards of the platoon position, Corporal Baldonado emplaced his weapon in an exposed position and delivered a withering stream of fire on the advancing enemy, causing them to fall back in disorder. The enemy then concentrated all their fire on Corporal Baldonado's gun and attempted to knock it out by rushing the position in small groups and hurling hand grenades. Several times, grenades exploded extremely close to Corporal Baldonado but failed to interrupt his continuous firing. The hostile troops made repeated attempts to storm his position and were driven back each time with appalling casualties. The enemy finally withdrew after making a final assault on Corporal Baldonado's position during which a grenade landed near his gun, killing him instantly. Corporal Baldonado's extraordinary heroism and selflessness at the cost of his own life, above and beyond the call of duty, are in keeping with the highest traditions of military service and reflect great credit upon himself, his unit, and the United States Army.

Espinosa, Victor H.*

Corporal Espinosa's military records were reviewed under the FY2002 National Defense Authorization Act, in which Congress requested that the DOD review service records of certain Jewish Americans or Hispanic Americans who had been awarded the Distinguished Service Cross, Navy Cross, or Air Force Cross.

Rank and organization: Corporal, U.S. Army. *Place and date:* Chorwon, Korea, August 1, 1952. *Entered service at:* Texas. *Born:* July 15,1929, El Paso, TX. *Date of issue:* March 18, 2014.

Citation: Corporal Victor H. Espinoza distinguished himself by acts of gallantry and intrepidity above and beyond the call of duty while serving as an acting rifleman in Company A, 23rd Infantry Regiment, 2nd Infantry Division during combat operations against an armed enemy in Chorwon, Korea, on August 1, 1952. On that day, Corporal Espinoza and his unit were responsible for securing and holding a vital enemy hill. As the friendly unit neared its objective, it was subjected to a devastating volume of enemy fire, slowing its progress. Corporal Espinoza, unhesitatingly and being fully aware of the hazards involved, left his place of comparative safety and made a deliberate one-man assault on the enemy with his rifle and grenades, destroying a machinegun and killing its crew. Corporal Espinoza continued across the fire-swept terrain to an exposed vantage point where he attacked an enemy mortar position and two bunkers with grenades and rifle fire, knocking out the enemy mortar position and destroying both bunkers and killing their occupants. Upon reaching the crest, and after running out of rifle ammunition, he called for more grenades. A comrade who was behind him threw some Chinese grenades to him. Immediately upon catching them, he pulled the pins and hurled them into the occupied trenches, killing and wounding more of the enemy with their own weapons. Continuing on through a tunnel, Corporal Espinoza made a daring charge, inflicting at least seven more casualties upon the enemy who were fast retreating into the tunnel. Corporal Espinoza was quickly in pursuit, but the hostile fire from the opening prevented him from overtaking the retreating enemy. As a result, Corporal Espinoza destroyed the tunnel with TNT, called for more grenades from his company, and hurled them at the enemy troops until they were out of reach. Corporal Espinoza's incredible display of valor secured the vital strong point and took a heavy toll on the enemy, resulting in at least 14 dead and 11 wounded. Corporal Espinoza's extraordinary heroism and selflessness above and beyond the call of duty are in keeping with the highest traditions of military service and reflect great credit upon himself, his unit, and the United States Army.

Gomez, Eduardo Corral*

Sergeant Gomez's military records were reviewed under the FY2002 National Defense Authorization Act, in which Congress requested that the DOD review service records of certain Jewish Americans or Hispanic Americans who had been awarded the Distinguished Service Cross, Navy Cross, or Air Force Cross.

Rank and organization: Sergeant First Class, Company 1, 8th Cavalry Regiment, 1st Cavalry Division, U.S. Army. *Place and date:* September 3, 1950, Tabu-dong, Korea. *Born:* October 28, 1919, Los Angeles, CA. *Date of issue:* March 18, 2014.

Citation: For conspicuous gallantry and intrepidity at the risk of his life above and beyond the call of duty:

Sergeant Eduardo C. Gomez distinguished himself by acts of gallantry and intrepidity above and beyond the call of duty while serving with Company I, 8th Cavalry Regiment, 1st Cavalry Division during combat operations against an armed enemy in Tabu-dong, Korea, on September 3, 1950. That afternoon, while conducting combat patrol, Sergeant Gomez's company was ruthlessly attacked by a hostile force that moved within 75 yards of the command post before it was immobilized by rocket fire. However, an enemy tank and multiple enemy machineguns continued to rake the company perimeter with devastating fire. Realizing the tank posed a serious threat to the entire perimeter, Sergeant Gomez voluntarily crawled 30 yards across an open rice field vulnerable to enemy observation and fire, boarded the tank, pried open one of the hatches on the turret, and dropped an activated grenade into the hull, killing the crew. Wounded in the left side while returning to his position, Sergeant Gomez refused evacuation. Observing that the tripod of a .30 caliber machinegun was rendered inoperable by enemy fire, he cradled the weapon in his arms, returned to the forward defensive positions, and swept the assaulting force with withering fire. Although his weapon overheated and burned his hands and his painful wound still bled, Sergeant Gomez maintained his stand and, upon orders to withdraw in the face of overwhelming enemy superiority, remained to provide protective fire. Sergeant Gomez continued to pour accurate fire into the enemy ranks, exacting a heavy toll in casualties and retarding their advance. Sergeant Gomez would not consent to leave his post for medical attention until the company established new defensive positions. Sergeant Gomez's extraordinary heroism and selflessness above and beyond the call of duty are in keeping with the highest traditions of military service and reflect great credit upon himself, his unit, and the United States Army.

Kaho'ohanohano, Anthony T.*

Private First Class Kaho'ohanohano's military records were among those reviewed under the FY2010 National Defense Authorization Act (P.L. 111-84, Title V, Subtitle F, Section 551). Following review, he was awarded the MOH.

Rank and organization: Private First Class, Company H, 17th Infantry Regiment, 7th Infantry Division, U.S. Army. *Place and date:* Chupa-ri, Korea, September 1, 1951. Entered service in Hawaii. *Born:* 1930. *Place of birth:* unknown. *Date of issue:* May 2, 2011.

Citation: For conspicuous gallantry and intrepidity at the risk of his life above and beyond the call of duty.

Private First Class Anthony T. Kaho'ohanohano, Company H, 17th Infantry Regiment, 7th Infantry Division, distinguished himself by extraordinary heroism in action against the enemy in the vicinity of Chupa-ri, Korea, on 1 September 1951. On that date, Private First Class Kaho'ohanohano was in charge of a machine-gun squad supporting the defensive positioning of Company F when a numerically superior enemy force launched a fierce attack. Because of the enemy's overwhelming numbers, friendly troops were forced to execute a limited withdrawal. As the men fell back, Private First Class Kaho'ohanohano ordered his squad to take up more defensible positions and provide covering fire for the withdrawing friendly force. Although having been wounded in the shoulder during the initial enemy assault, Private First Class Kaho'ohanohano gathered a supply of grenades and ammunition and returned to his original position to face the enemy alone. As the hostile troops concentrated their strength against his emplacement in an effort to overrun it, Private First Class Kaho'ohanohano fought fiercely and courageously, delivering deadly accurate fire into the ranks of the onrushing enemy. When his ammunition was depleted, he engaged the enemy in hand-to-hand combat until he was killed. Private First Class Kaho'ohanohano's heroic stand so inspired his comrades that they launched a counterattack that completely repulsed the enemy. Upon reaching Private First Class Kaho'ohanohano's emplacement, friendly troops discovered 11 enemy soldiers lying dead in front of the emplacement and two inside it, killed in hand-to-hand combat. Private First Class Kaho'ohanohano's extraordinary heroism and selfless devotion to duty are in keeping with the finest traditions of military service and reflect great credit upon himself, the 7th Infantry Division, and the United States Army.

Kapaun, Emil Joseph.*

Congress, in the National Defense Authorization Act for Fiscal Year 2012, (P.L. 112-81, Title V, Subtitle I, Section 594, authorized the President to award the MOH posthumously to Captain Emil Joseph Kapaun, upgrading his Distinguished Service Cross.[13]

Rank and organization: Captain (Chaplain), 3rd Battalion, 8th Cavalry Regiment, 1st Cavalry Division, U.S. Army. *Place and date:* Unsan, Korea, November 1-2, 1950. *Entered service at:* Kansas. *Born:* April 20, 1916, Pilsen, KS. *Date of issue:* April 11, 2013.

Citation: For conspicuous gallantry and intrepidity at the risk of his life above and beyond the call of duty while serving with the 3rd Battalion, 8th Cavalry Regiment, 1st Cavalry Division during combat operations against an armed enemy at Unsan, Korea, from November 1-2, 1950.

On November 1, as Chinese Communist Forces viciously attacked friendly elements, Chaplain Kapaun calmly walked through withering enemy fire in order to provide comfort and medical aid to his comrades and rescue friendly wounded from no-man's land. Though the Americans successfully repelled the assault, they found themselves surrounded by the enemy. Facing annihilation, the able-bodied men were ordered to evacuate. However, Chaplain Kapaun, fully aware of his certain capture, elected to stay behind with the wounded. After the enemy succeeded in breaking through the defense in the early morning hours of November 2, Chaplain Kapaun continually made rounds, as hand-to-hand combat ensued. As Chinese Communist Forces approached the American position, Chaplain Kapaun noticed an injured Chinese officer amongst

---

[13] *Army*, "Father Emil Kapaun, at http://www.ausa.org/publications/armymagazine/archive/2012/11/Documents/Latham_1112.pdf.

the wounded and convinced him to negotiate the safe surrender of the American Forces. Shortly after his capture, Chaplain Kapaun, with complete disregard for his personal safety and unwavering resolve, bravely pushed aside an enemy soldier preparing to execute Sergeant First Class Herbert A. Miller. Not only did Chaplain Kapaun's gallantry save the life of Sergeant Miller, but also his unparalleled courage and leadership inspired all those present, including those who might have otherwise fled in panic, to remain and fight the enemy until captured. Chaplain Kapaun's extraordinary heroism and selflessness, above and beyond the call of duty, are in keeping with the highest traditions of military service and reflect great credit upon himself, the 3rd Battalion, 8th Cavalry Regiment, the 1st Cavalry Division, and the United States Army. President Barack Obama presented the Medal of Honor to Kapaun's nephew at the White House on April 11, 2013.

Keeble, Woodrow W.

Congress approved Supplemental Appropriations for Defense, International Affairs, and other Security Related Needs[14] on May 25, 2007, removing the statutory time limit on the award for Master Sergeant Keeble.

Rank and organization: Master Sergeant, Company G, 2nd Battalion, 19th Infantry Regiment, 24th Infantry Division, U.S. Army. *Place and date:* Sangsan-ni, Korea, October 20, 1951. *Entered service at:* Wahpeton, ND. *Born:* May 16, 1917, Waubay, SD. *Date of issue:* March 3, 2008.

Citation: For conspicuous gallantry and intrepidity at the risk of his life above and beyond the call of duty.

Master Sergeant Woodrow W. Keeble distinguished himself by acts of gallantry and intrepidity above and beyond the call of duty in action with an armed enemy near Sangsan-ni, Korea, on October 20, 1951. On that day, Master Sergeant Keeble was an acting platoon leader for the support platoon in Company G, 19th Infantry, in the attack on Hill 765, a steep and rugged position that was well defended by the enemy. Leading the support platoon, Master Sergeant Keeble saw that the attacking elements had become pinned down on the slope by heavy enemy fire from three well-fortified and strategically placed enemy positions. With complete disregard for his personal safety, Master Sergeant Keeble dashed forward and joined the pinned-down platoon. Then, hugging the ground, Master Sergeant Keeble crawled forward alone until he was in close proximity to one of the hostile machine-gun emplacements. Ignoring the heavy fire that the crew trained on him, Master Sergeant Keeble activated a grenade and threw it with great accuracy, successfully destroying the position. Continuing his one-man assault, he moved to the second enemy position and destroyed it with another grenade. Despite the fact that the enemy troops were now directing their firepower against him and unleashing a shower of grenades in a frantic attempt to stop his advance, he moved forward against the third hostile emplacement, and skillfully neutralized the remaining enemy position. As his comrades moved forward to join him, Master Sergeant Keeble continued to direct accurate fire against nearby trenches, inflicting heavy casualties on the enemy. Inspired by his courage, Company G successfully moved forward and seized its important objective. The extraordinary courage, selfless service, and devotion to duty displayed that day by Master Sergeant Keeble was an inspiration to all around him and reflected great credit upon himself, his unit, and the United States Army.

---

[14] P.L. 110-28, Section 3308 (a).

Kravitz, Leonard M.*

Private Kravitz's military records were reviewed under the FY2002 National Defense Authorization Act, P.L. 107-107, Section 551, on December 28, 2001, in which Congress requested that the DOD review service records of certain Jewish Americans or Hispanic Americans who had been awarded the Distinguished Service Cross, Navy Cross, or Air Force Cross.

Rank and organization: Private First Class, Company M, 3rd Battalion, 5th Infantry Regiment, U.S. Army. *Place and date:* Yangpyong, Korea, March 6-7, 1951. *Entered service at:* New York. *Born:* 1931, Brooklyn, NY. *Date of issue:* March 18, 2014.

Citation: For conspicuous gallantry and intrepidity at the risk of his life above and beyond the call of duty:

Private First Class Leonard M. Kravitz distinguished himself by acts of gallantry and intrepidity above and beyond the call of duty while serving as an assistant machinegunner with Company M, 5th Infantry Regiment, 24th Infantry Division during combat operations against an armed enemy in Yangpyong, Korea, on March 6 and 7, 1951. After friendly elements had repulsed two probing attacks, the enemy launched a fanatical banzai charge with heavy supporting fire and, despite staggering losses, pressed the assault with ruthless determination. When the machinegunner was wounded in the initial phase of the action, Private First Class Kravitz immediately seized the weapon and poured devastating fire into the ranks of the onrushing assailants. The enemy effected and exploited a breach on the left flank, rendering the friendly positions untenable. Upon order to withdraw, Private First Class Kravitz voluntarily remained to provide protective fire for the retiring elements. Detecting enemy troops moving toward friendly positions, Private First Class Kravitz swept the hostile soldiers with deadly, accurate fire, killing the entire group. His destructive retaliation caused the enemy to concentrate vicious fire on his position and enabled the friendly elements to withdraw. Later, after friendly troops had returned, Private First Class Kravitz was found dead behind the gun he had so heroically manned, surrounded by numerous enemy dead. Private First Class Kravitz's extraordinary heroism and selflessness at the cost of his own life, above and beyond the call of duty, are in keeping with the highest traditions of military service and reflect great credit upon himself, his unit, and the United States Army.

Negron, Juan E.

Sergeant Negron's military records were reviewed under the FY2002 National Defense Authorization Act, in which Congress requested that the DOD review service records of certain Jewish Americans or Hispanic Americans who had been awarded the Distinguished Service Cross, Navy Cross, or Air Force Cross.

Rank and organization: Sergeant, U.S. Army. *Place and date:* Kalma-Eri, Korea, April 28, 1951. *Born:* September 26, 1929, Corozal, Puerto Rico. *Date of issue:* March 18, 2014.

Citation: For conspicuous gallantry and intrepidity at the risk of his life above and beyond the call of duty:

Sergeant Juan E. Negron distinguished himself by acts of gallantry and intrepidity above and beyond the call of duty while serving as a member of Company L, 65th Infantry Regiment, 3rd Infantry Division during combat operations against an armed enemy in Kalma-Eri, Korea, on April 28, 1951. That afternoon, Sergeant Negron took up the most vulnerable position on his company's exposed right flank after an enemy force had overrun a section of the line. When notified that elements of his company were withdrawing, Sergeant Negron refused to leave his exposed position, instead delivering withering fire at hostile troops who had broken through a road block. When the hostile troops approached his position, Sergeant Negron accurately hurled hand grenades at short range, halting their attack. Sergeant Negron held the position throughout the night while friendly forces organized and launched a counterattack. The next morning, after the enemy had been repulsed, friendly forces relieved Sergeant Negron and found the bodies of 15 enemy soldiers surrounding his position. Sergeant Negron's extraordinary heroism and selflessness above and beyond the call of duty are in keeping with the highest traditions of military service and reflect great credit upon himself, his unit, and the United States Army.

Pena, Mike C.*

Sergeant Pena's military records were reviewed under the FY2002 National Defense Authorization Act, in which Congress requested that the DOD review service records of certain Jewish Americans or Hispanic Americans who had been awarded the Distinguished Service Cross, Navy Cross, or Air Force Cross.

Rank and organization: Master Sergeant, Company F, 2nd Battalion, 5th Cavalry Regiment, 1st Cavalry Division, U.S. Army. *Place and date:* Waegwan, Korea, September 4, 1950. *Entered service at:* El Paso, TX. *Born:* November 6, 1924, Newgulf, TX. *Date of issue:* March 18, 2014.

Citation: For conspicuous gallantry and intrepidity at the risk of his life above and beyond the call of duty:

Master Sergeant Mike C. Pena distinguished himself by acts of gallantry and intrepidity above and beyond the call of duty while serving as a member of Company F, 5th Cavalry Regiment, 1st Cavalry Division during combat operations against an armed enemy in Waegwan, Korea, on September 4, 1950. That evening, under cover of darkness and a dreary mist, an enemy battalion moved to within a few yards of Master Sergeant Pena's platoon. Recognizing the enemy's approach, Master Sergeant Pena and his men opened fire, but the enemy's sudden emergence and accurate, point-blank fire forced the friendly troops to withdraw. Master Sergeant Pena rapidly reorganized his men and led them in a counterattack, which succeeded in regaining the positions they had just lost. He and his men quickly established a defensive perimeter and laid down devastating fire, but enemy troops continued to hurl themselves at the defenses in overwhelming numbers. Realizing that their scarce supply of ammunition would soon make their positions untenable, Master Sergeant Pena ordered his men to fall back and manned a machinegun to cover their withdrawal. He singlehandedly held back the enemy until the early hours of the following morning when his position was overrun and he was killed. Master Sergeant Pena's extraordinary heroism and selflessness at the cost of his own life, above and beyond the call of duty, are in keeping with the highest traditions of military service and reflect great credit upon himself, his unit, and the United States Army.

Rivera, Demensio*

Private Rivera's military records were reviewed under the FY2002 National Defense Authorization Act, in which Congress requested that the DOD review service records of certain Jewish Americans or Hispanic Americans who had been awarded the Distinguished Service Cross, Navy Cross, or Air Force Cross.

Rank and organization: Private, Company G, 2nd Battalion, 7th Infantry Regiment, 3rd Infantry Division, U.S. Army. *Place and date:* Changyongni, Korea, May 22-23, 1951. *Entered service at:* New York. *Born:* 29 April 1933, Cabo Rojo, Puerto Rico. *Date of issue:* March 18, 2014.

Citation: For conspicuous gallantry and intrepidity at the risk of his life above and beyond the call of duty:

Private Demensio Rivera distinguished himself by acts of gallantry and intrepidity above and beyond the call of duty while serving as an automatic rifleman with 2nd Platoon, Company G, 7th Infantry Regiment, 3rd Infantry Division during combat operations against an armed enemy in Changyong-ni, Korea, on May 23, 1951. Early that morning, a large hostile force emerged from a dense fog and viciously attacked Private Rivera and his comrades. Private Rivera immediately responded by firing with deadly accuracy until his weapon jammed. Without hesitating, he threw his rifle down and began to engage the enemy with his pistol and grenades. At one point, Private Rivera fearlessly crawled from his emplacement to engage an infiltrating enemy soldier in fierce hand-to-hand combat. With only the sound of footsteps and obscure shadows to guide his aim, Private Rivera held his position against tremendous odds, inflicting numerous casualties on the enemy until he found himself without ammunition of any kind except one grenade. Displaying a peerless fighting spirit and an utterly selfless devotion to duty, Private Rivera pulled the pin from his last grenade and calmly waited for the enemy to reach his position. As enemy troops leaped inside his bunker, Private Rivera activated the grenade with the full knowledge that it meant his almost certain death. When the debris from the explosion had cleared, friendly forces recovered a severely wounded Private Rivera and discovered the bodies of four dead or dying enemy soldiers surrounding him. Private Rivera's extraordinary heroism and selflessness above and beyond the call of duty are in keeping with the highest traditions of military service and reflect great credit upon himself, his unit, and the United States Army.

Rubin, Tibor

Rank and organization: Corporal, U.S. Army. *Place and date:* Republic of Korea, July 23, 1950 to April 20, 1953. *Entered service at:* unknown. *Born:* 18 June 1929, Hungary. *Date of issue:* September 23, 2005.

Citation: For conspicuous gallantry and intrepidity at the risk of his life above and beyond the call of duty.

Corporal Tibor Rubin distinguished himself by extraordinary heroism during the period from July 23, 1950, to April 20, 1953, while serving as a rifleman with Company I, 8th Cavalry Regiment, 1st Cavalry Division in the Republic of Korea. While his unit was retreating to the Pusan Perimeter, Corporal Rubin was assigned to stay behind to keep open the vital Taegu-Pusan Road link used by his withdrawing unit. During the ensuing battle, overwhelming numbers of North Korean troops assaulted a hill defended solely by Corporal Rubin. He inflicted a staggering number of casualties on the attacking force during his personal 24-hour battle, single-handedly slowing the enemy advance and allowing the 8th Cavalry Regiment to complete its withdrawal successfully. Following the breakout from the Pusan Perimeter, the 8th Cavalry Regiment proceeded northward and advanced into North Korea. During the advance, he helped capture several hundred North Korean soldiers. On October 30, 1950, Chinese forces attacked his unit at Unsan, North Korea, during a massive nighttime assault. That night and throughout the next day, he manned a .30 caliber machine gun at the south end of the unit's line after three previous gunners became casualties. He continued to man his machine gun until his ammunition was exhausted. His determined stand slowed the pace of the enemy advance in his sector, permitting the remnants of his unit to retreat southward. As the battle raged, Corporal Rubin was severely wounded and captured by the Chinese. Choosing to remain in the prison camp despite offers from the Chinese to return him to his native Hungary, Corporal Rubin disregarded his own personal safety and immediately began sneaking out of the camp at night in search of food for his comrades. Breaking into enemy food storehouses and gardens, he risked certain torture or death if caught. Corporal Rubin provided not only food to the starving Soldiers, but also desperately needed medical care and moral support for the sick and wounded of the POW camp. His brave, selfless efforts were directly attributed to saving the lives of as many as forty of his fellow prisoners. Corporal Rubin's gallant actions in close contact with the enemy and unyielding courage and bravery while a prisoner of war are in the highest traditions of military service and reflect great credit upon himself and the United States Army.

Svehla, Henry*

Private First Class Svehla's military records were among those reviewed at the request of Congress. Following review, he was awarded the MOH, an upgrade from his Distinguished Service Cross.

Rank and Organization: Private First Class, F Company, 32nd Infantry Regiment, 7th Infantry Division, U.S. Army. *Place and date:* Pyongong, Korea, 12 June, 1952. *Entered service at:* New Jersey. *Born:* 1932, New Jersey. *Date of issue:* May 2, 2011.

Citation: Private First Class Henry Svehla distinguished himself by acts of gallantry and intrepidity above and beyond the call of duty while serving as a Rifleman with F Company, 32d Infantry Regiment, 7th Infantry Division, in connection with combat operations against an armed enemy in Pyongong, Korea, on 12 June 1952.

That afternoon while Private First Class Svehla and his platoon were patrolling a strategic hill to determine enemy strength and positions, they were subjected to intense enemy automatic weapons and small arms fire at the top of the hill. Coming under the heavy fire, the platoon's attack began to falter. Realizing the success of the mission and the safety of the remaining troops were in peril, Private First Class Svehla leapt to his feet and charged the enemy positions, firing his weapon and throwing grenades as he advanced. In the face of this courage and determination, the platoon rallied to the attack with renewed vigor. Private First Class Svehla, utterly disregarding his own safety, destroyed enemy positions and inflicted heavy casualties, when suddenly fragments from a mortar round exploding nearby seriously wounded him in the face. Despite his wounds, Private First Class Svehla refused medical treatment and continued to lead the attack. When an enemy grenade landed among a group of his comrades, Private First Class Svehla, without hesitation and undoubtedly aware of the extreme danger, threw himself upon the grenade. During this action, Private First Class Svehla was mortally wounded. Private First Class Svehla's extraordinary heroism and selflessness at the cost of his own life, above and beyond the call of duty, are in keeping with the highest traditions of the military service and reflect great credit upon himself, his unit, and the United States Army.

Vera, Miguel Armando*

Private Vera's military records were reviewed under the FY2002 National Defense Authorization Act, P.L. 107-107, Section 552. P.L. 107-107 requested that the DOD review service records of certain Jewish Americans or Hispanic Americans who had been awarded the Distinguished Service Cross, Navy Cross, or Air Force Cross.

Rank and organization: Private, Company F, 2nd Battalion, 38th Infantry Regiment, 2nd Infantry Division, U.S. Army. *Place and date:* Chorwon, Korea, September 21, 1952. *Born:* May 3, 1932, Puerto Rico. *Date of issue:* March 18, 2014.

Citation: For conspicuous gallantry and intrepidity at the risk of his life above and beyond the call of duty:

Private Miguel A. Vera distinguished himself by acts of gallantry and intrepidity above and beyond the call of duty while serving as an automatic rifleman with Company F, 38th Infantry 2nd Infantry Division in Chorwon, Korea, on September 21, 1952. That morning, despite suffering from wounds inflicted in a previous battle, Private Vera voluntarily left the aid station to join his comrades in an attack against well-fortified enemy positions on a hill of great importance. When the assaulting elements had moved within 20 yards of the enemy positions, they were suddenly trapped by a heavy volume of mortar, artillery, and small-arms fire. The company prepared to make a limited withdrawal, but Private Vera volunteered to remain behind to provide covering fire. As his companions moved to safety, Private Vera remained steadfast in his position, directing accurate fire against the hostile positions despite the intense volume of fire that the enemy was concentrating upon him. Later in the morning, when the friendly force returned, they discovered Private Vera in the same position, facing the enemy. Private Vera's noble intrepidity and self-sacrifice saved many of his comrades' lives. Private Vera's extraordinary heroism and selflessness at the cost of his own life, above and beyond the call of duty, are in keeping with the highest traditions of the military service and reflect great credit upon himself, his unit, and the United States Army.

Weinstein, Jack*

Sergeant Weinstein's military records were reviewed under the FY2002 National Defense Authorization Act, P.L. 107-107, Section 552. P.L. 107-107 requested that the DOD review service records of certain Jewish Americans or Hispanic Americans who had been awarded the Distinguished Service Cross, Navy Cross, or Air Force Cross.

Rank and organization: Sergeant, Company G, 21st Infantry Regiment, U.S. Army. *Place and date:* Kumson, Korea, October 19, 1951. *Born:* October 18, 1928, Lamar, MO. *Date of issue:* March 18, 2014.

Citation: For conspicuous gallantry and intrepidity at the risk of his life above and beyond the call of duty:

Sergeant Jack Weinstein distinguished himself by acts of gallantry and intrepidity above and beyond the call of duty while leading 1st Platoon, Company G, 21st Infantry Regiment, 24th Infantry Division in Kumsong, Korea, on October 19, 1951. That afternoon, 30 enemy troops counterattacked Sergeant Weinstein's platoon. Most of the platoon's members had been wounded in the previous action and withdrew under the heavy fire. Sergeant Weinstein, however, remained in his position and continued to fight off the onrushing enemy, killing at least six with his M-1 rifle before running out of ammunition. Although under extremely heavy enemy fire, Sergeant Weinstein refused to withdraw and continued fighting by throwing enemy hand grenades found lying near his position. He again halted the enemy's progress and inflicted numerous casualties. Alone and unaided, he held the ground that his platoon had fought tenaciously to take and held out against overwhelming odds until another platoon was able to relieve him and drive back the enemy. Sergeant Weinstein's leg had been broken by an enemy grenade and old wounds suffered in previous battles had reopened, but he refused to withdraw and successfully bought time for his wounded comrades to reach friendly lines. Sergeant Weinstein's extraordinary heroism and selflessness above and beyond the call of duty are in keeping with the highest traditions of the military service and reflect great credit upon himself, his unit, and the United States Army.

Vietnam War

Adkins, Bennie G.

In H.R. 3304, the National Defense Authorization Act for Fiscal Year 2014, P.L. 113-66, Congress authorized the President of the United States to award the MOH to Command Sergeant Adkins, waiving time limitations found in 10 U.S.C. § 3744.

Rank and organization: Command Sergeant Major, Detachment A-102, 5th Special Forces Group, 1st Special Forces. *Place and date:* Camp A Shau, Republic of Vietnam, March 9-12, 1966. *Entered service at:* unknown. *Born:. Date of issue:* September 15, 2014.

Sergeant First Class Adkins distinguished himself during the period March 9, 1966, to March 12, 1966, during combat operations at Camp A Shau, Republic of Vietnam. When the camp was attacked by a large Viet Cong force, Sergeant First Class Adkins rushed through intense hostile fire and manned a mortar position. Although he was wounded, he ran through exploding mortar rounds and dragged several of his comrades to safety. When the hostile fire subsided, Sergeant First Class Adkins exposed himself to sporadic sniper fire and carried his wounded comrades to the camp dispensary. During the evacuation of a seriously wounded American, Sergeant First Class Adkins maneuvered outside the camp walls to draw fire and successfully covered the rescue. During the early morning hours of March 10, 1966, a Viet Cong regiment launched its main attack. Within two hours, Sergeant First Class Adkins was the only man firing a mortar weapon. Although he was painfully wounded and most of his crew was killed or wounded, he fought off the fanatical waves of attacking Viet Cong. After withdrawing to a communications bunker where several Americans were attempting to fight off a company of Viet Cong, Sergeant First Class Adkins killed numerous insurgents with his suppressive fire. Running extremely low on ammunition, he returned to the mortar pit, gathered the vital ammunition, and ran through intense fire back to the communications bunker. After being ordered to evacuate the camp, all signal equipment and classified documents were destroyed. Sergeant First Class Adkins and a small group of men fought their way out of the camp and evaded the Viet Cong for two days until they were rescued by a helicopter. Sergeant First Class Adkins's extraordinary heroism in close combat against a numerically superior hostile force was in keeping with the highest traditions of the military service and reflect great credit upon himself, his unit, and the United States Army.

Alvarado, Leonard L.*

Specialist Alvarado's military records were reviewed under the FY2002 National Defense Authorization Act, in which Congress requested that the DOD review service records of certain Jewish Americans or Hispanic Americans who had been awarded the Distinguished Service Cross, Navy Cross, or Air Force Cross.

Rank and organization: Specialist Fourth Class, U.S. Army. *Place and date:* Phuoc Long Province, Republic of Vietnam, August 12, 1969. *Entered service at:* Bakersfield, CA. *Born:* February 13, 1947, Bakersfield, California. *Date of issue:* March 18, 2014.

Citation: For conspicuous gallantry and intrepidity at the risk of his life above and beyond the call of duty:

Specialist Four Leonard L. Alvarado distinguished himself by acts of gallantry and intrepidity above and beyond the call of duty while serving as a rifleman with Company D, 2nd Battalion, 12th Cavalry, 1st Cavalry Division (Airmobile) during combat operations against an armed enemy in Phuoc Long Province, Republic of Vietnam on August 12, 1969. On that day, as Specialist Four Alvarado and a small reaction force moved through dense jungle en route to a beleaguered friendly platoon, Specialist Four Alvarado detected enemy movement and opened fire. Despite his quick reaction, Specialist Four Alvarado and his comrades were soon pinned down by the hostile force that blocked the path to the trapped platoon. Specialist Four Alvarado quickly moved forward through the hostile machinegun fire in order to engage the enemy troops. Suddenly, an enemy grenade exploded nearby, wounding and momentarily stunning him. Retaliating immediately, he killed the grenadier just as another enemy barrage wounded him again. Specialist Four Alvarado crawled forward through the fusillade to pull several comrades back within the hastily formed perimeter. Realizing his element needed to break away from the hostile force, Specialist Four Alvarado began maneuvering forward alone. Though repeatedly thrown to the ground by exploding satchel charges, he continued advancing and firing, silencing several emplacements, including one enemy machinegun position. From his dangerous forward position, he persistently laid suppressive fire on the hostile forces, and after the enemy troops had broken contact, his comrades discovered that he had succumbed to his wounds. Specialist Four Alvarado's extraordinary heroism and selflessness at the cost of his own life, above and beyond the call of duty, are in keeping with the highest traditions of military service and reflect great credit upon himself, his unit, and the United States Army.

Benavidez, Roy P.

Congress approved P.L. 96-81, December 18, 1980, removing the statutory time limit on the award for Master Sergeant Benavidez.

Rank and organization: Master Sergeant, Detachment B-56, Fifth Special Forces Group, Republic of Vietnam. *Place and date:* West of Loc Ninh on 2 May 1968. *Entered service at:* Houston, TX, June 1955. *Born:* 5 August 1935, DeWitt County, Cuero, TX. *Date of issue:* February 24, 1981.[15]

Citation: Master Sergeant (then Staff Sergeant) Roy P. Benavidez, United States Army, who distinguished himself by a series of daring and extremely valorous actions on 2 May 1968 while assigned to Detachment B 56, Fifth Special Forces Group (Airborne), First Special Forces, Republic of Vietnam.

On the morning of 2 May 1968, a 12-man Special Forces Reconnaissance Team was inserted by helicopters in a dense jungle area west of Loc Ninh, Vietnam, to gather intelligence information about confirmed large-scale enemy activity. This area was controlled and routinely patrolled by the North Vietnamese Army. After a short period of time on the ground, the team met heavy enemy resistance, and requested emergency extraction. Three helicopters attempted extraction, but were unable to land due to intense enemy small arms and anti-aircraft fire. Sergeant Benavidez was at the Forward Operating Base in Loc Ninh monitoring the operation by radio when these helicopters returned to off-load wounded crew members and to assess aircraft damage. Sergeant Benavidez voluntarily boarded a returning aircraft to assist in another extraction attempt. Realizing that all the team members were either dead or wounded and unable to move to the pickup zone, he directed the aircraft to a nearby clearing, where he jumped from the hovering helicopter and ran approximately 75 meters under withering small arms fire to the crippled team. Prior to reaching the team's position he was wounded in his right leg, face, and head. Despite these painful injuries, he took charge, repositioning the team members and directing their fire to facilitate the landing of an extraction aircraft, and the loading of wounded and dead team members. He then threw smoke canisters to direct the aircraft to the team's position. Despite his severe wounds and under intense enemy fire, he carried and dragged half of the wounded team members to the awaiting aircraft. He then provided protective fire by running alongside the aircraft as it moved to pick up the remaining team members. As the enemy's fire intensified, he hurried to recover the body and classified documents on the dead team leader. When he reached the leader's body, Sergeant Benavidez was severely wounded by small arms fire in the abdomen and grenade fragments in his back. At nearly the same moment, the aircraft pilot was mortally wounded, and his helicopter crashed. Although in extremely critical condition due to his multiple wounds, Sergeant Benavidez secured the classified documents and made his way back to the wreckage, where he aided the wounded out of the overturned aircraft, and gathered

---

[15] *Washington Post*, "President Awards Medal," February 25, 1981.

the stunned survivors into a defensive perimeter. Under increasing enemy automatic weapons and grenade fire, he moved around the perimeter distributing water and ammunition to his weary men, re-instilling in them a will to live and fight. Facing a buildup of enemy opposition with a beleaguered team, Sergeant Benavidez mustered his strength, began calling in tactical air strikes, and directed the fire from supporting gunships to suppress the enemy's fire and so permit another extraction attempt. He was wounded again in his thigh by small arms fire while administering first aid to a wounded team member just before another extraction helicopter was able to land. His indomitable spirit kept him going as he began to ferry his comrades to the craft. On his second trip with the wounded, he was clubbed from additional wounds to his head and arms[16] before killing his adversary. He then continued under devastating fire to carry the wounded to the helicopter. Upon reaching the aircraft, he spotted and killed two enemy soldiers who were rushing the craft from an angle that prevented the aircraft door gunner from firing upon them. With little strength remaining, he made one last trip to the perimeter to ensure that all classified material had been collected or destroyed, and to bring in the remaining wounded. Only then, in extremely serious condition from numerous wounds and loss of blood, did he allow himself to be pulled into the extraction aircraft. Sergeant Benavidez's gallant choice to join voluntarily his comrades who were in critical straits, to expose himself constantly to withering enemy fire, and his refusal to be stopped despite numerous severe wounds, saved the lives of at least eight men.

His fearless personal leadership, tenacious devotion to duty, and extremely valorous actions in the face of overwhelming odds were in keeping with the highest traditions of the military service, and reflect the utmost credit on him and the United States Army.

Conde-Falcon, Felix M.*

Staff Sergeant Conde-Falcon's military records were reviewed under the FY2002 National Defense Authorization Act, P.L. 107-107, Section 552. P.L. 107-107 requested that the DOD review service records of certain Jewish Americans or Hispanic Americans who had been awarded the Distinguished Service Cross, Navy Cross, or Air Force Cross.

Rank and organization: Staff Sergeant, Company D, 1st Battalion, 505th Infantry Regiment, 3rd Brigade, 82nd Airborne Division, U.S. Army. *Place and date:* Ap Tan Hoa, Republic of Vietnam, April 4, 1969. *Entered service at:* Chicago, IL. *Born:* February 24, 1938, Juncos, Puerto Rico. *Date of issue:* March 18, 2014.

Citation: For conspicuous gallantry and intrepidity at the risk of his life above and beyond the call of duty:

Staff Sergeant Felix M. Conde-Falcon distinguished himself by acts of gallantry and intrepidity above and beyond the call of duty while serving as an acting Platoon Leader in Company D, 1st Battalion, 505th Infantry Regiment, 3rd Brigade, 82nd Airborne Division during combat operations against an armed enemy in Ap Tan Hoa, Republic of Vietnam, on April 4, 1969. While entering a heavily wooded section on the route of advance, Staff Sergeant Conde-Falcon and his company encountered an extensive enemy bunker complex, later identified as a battalion command post. Following tactical artillery and air strikes on the heavily secured enemy position, Staff Sergeant Conde-Falcon's platoon was selected to assault and clear the bunker fortifications. Moving out ahead of his platoon, Staff Sergeant Conde-Falcon charged the first bunker, heaving grenades as he went. As the hostile fire increased, he crawled to the blind side of an entrenchment position, jumped to the roof, and tossed a grenade into the bunker aperture. Without hesitating, he

---

[16] Omission of words in this phrase occurred in the original official citation.

proceeded to two additional bunkers, both of which he destroyed in the same manner as the first. Rejoining his platoon, Staff Sergeant Conde-Falcon advanced about one hundred meters through the trees before coming under intense hostile fire. Selecting three men to accompany him, he maneuvered toward the enemy's flank position. Carrying a machinegun, he singlehandedly assaulted the nearest fortification, killing the enemy inside before running out of ammunition. After returning to the three men with his empty weapon and taking up an M-16 rifle, he concentrated on the next bunker. Within 10 meters of his goal, Staff Sergeant Conde-Falcon was shot by an unseen assailant and soon died of his wounds. Staff Sergeant Conde-Falcon's extraordinary heroism and selflessness at the cost of his own life, above and beyond the call of duty, are in keeping with the highest traditions of military service and reflect great credit upon himself, his unit, and the United States Army.

Cook, Donald G.*

Colonel Cook received his MOH for his heroic behavior while being held as a POW in North Vietnam. News of his deeds could not be obtained until POWs with whom he had served were repatriated. The law provides that time limitations may be waived in such cases.[17]

Rank and organization: Colonel, U.S. Marine Corps. *Place and date:* Binh Gia, Phovc Tuy Province, South Vietnam, December 31, 1964. *Entered service at:* Quantico, Virginia. *Born:* August 9, 1934, Brooklyn, NY. *Date of issue:* May 16, 1980.[18]

Citation: For conspicuous gallantry and intrepidity at the risk of his life above and beyond the call of duty while interned as Prisoner of War by the Viet Cong in the Republic of Vietnam during the period 31 December 1964 to 8 December 1967.

Despite the fact that by so doing he knew he would bring about harsher treatment for himself, Colonel (then Captain) Cook established himself as the senior prisoner, even though in actuality he was not. Repeatedly assuming more than his share of the manual labor in order that the Prisoners of War could improve the state of their health, Colonel Cook willingly and unselfishly put the interests of his comrades before that of his own well-being and, eventually, his life. Giving more needy men his medicine and drug allowance while constantly nursing them, he risked infection from contagious diseases while in a rapidly deteriorating state of health. This unselfish and exemplary conduct, coupled with his refusal to stray even the slightest from the Code of Conduct, earned him the deepest respect from not only his fellow prisoners, but his captors as well. Rather than negotiate for his own release or better treatment, he steadfastly frustrated attempts by the Viet Cong to break his indomitable spirit, and passed this same resolve on to the men with whose well-being he so closely associated himself. Knowing his refusals would prevent his release prior to the end of the war, and also knowing his chances for prolonged survival would be small in the event of continued refusal, he chose nevertheless to adhere to a Code of Conduct far above that which could be expected.

His personal valor and exceptional spirit of loyalty in the face of almost certain death reflected the highest credit upon Colonel Cook, the Marine Corps, and the United States Naval Service.

---

[17] 10 U.S.C. §3744, 6248, 8744.

[18] *Washington Post*, "Marine Who Gave Life Is Awarded Medal," May 17, 1980.

Copas, Ardie R.*

Specialist Copas's military records were reviewed under the FY2002 National Defense Authorization Act, P.L. 107-107, Section 552. P.L. 107-107 requested that the DODreview service records of certain Jewish Americans or Hispanic Americans who had been awarded the Distinguished Service Cross, Navy Cross, or Air Force Cross.

Rank and organization: Specialist Fourth Class, Company C, 1st Battalion (Mechanized), 5th Infantry Regiment, 25th Infantry Division, U.S. Army. *Place and date:* Ph Romeas Hek, Cambodia, May 12, 1970. *Entered service at:* Fort Pierce, FL. *Born:* Fort Pierce, FL, August 29, 1950. *Date of issue:* March 18, 2014.

Citation: For conspicuous gallantry and intrepidity at the risk of his life above and beyond the call of duty:

Specialist Four Ardie R. Copas distinguished himself by acts of gallantry and intrepidity above and beyond the call of duty while serving as a Machinegunner in Company C, 1st Battalion (Mechanized), 5th Infantry Regiment, 25th Infantry Division during combat operations against an armed enemy near Ph Romeas Hek, Cambodia, on May 12, 1970. That morning, Specialist Four Copas's company was suddenly attacked by a large hostile force firing recoilless rifles, rocket-propelled grenades, and automatic weapons. As Specialist Four Copas began returning fire, his armored car was struck by an enemy recoilless round, knocking him to the ground and injuring four American soldiers beside the vehicle. Ignoring his own wounds, Specialist Four Copas quickly remounted the burning vehicle and commenced firing his machinegun at the belligerents. Braving the hostile fire directed at him and the possible detonation of the mortar rounds inside the track, Specialist Four Copas maintained a heavy volume of suppressive fire on the foe while the wounded Americans were safely evacuated. Undaunted, Specialist Four Copas continued to place devastating volleys of fire upon the adversary until he was mortally wounded when another enemy round hit his vehicle. Specialist Four Copas's daring action resulted in the safe evacuation of his comrades. Specialist Four Copas's extraordinary heroism and selflessness at the cost of his own life, above and beyond the call of duty, are in keeping with the highest traditions of military service and reflect great credit upon himself, his unit, and the United States Army.

Crandall, Bruce P.

Congress approved the FY1996 National Defense Authorization Act, P.L. 104-106, Section 522, on February 10, 1996, waiving the statutory time limit on any award or decoration for an act of valor performed while serving on active duty during the Vietnam era.

Rank and Organization: Major, Company A, 229th Assault Helicopter Battalion, 1st Cavalry Division (Airmobile), U.S. Army. *Place and date:* Ia Drang Valley, Republic of Vietnam, November 14, 1965. *Place and date of birth:* Olympia, WA, 1933. *Date of issue:* February 26, 2007.

Citation: For conspicuous gallantry and intrepidity at the risk of his life above and beyond the call of duty: Major Bruce P. Crandall distinguished himself by extraordinary heroism as a Flight Commander in the Republic of Vietnam, while serving with Company A, 229th Assault Helicopter Battalion, 1st Cavalry Division (Airmobile).

On 14 November 1965, his flight of 16 helicopters was lifting troops for a search and destroy mission from Plei Me, Vietnam, to Landing Zone X-Ray in the Ia Drang Valley. On the fourth troop lift, the airlift began to take enemy fire, and by the time the aircraft had refueled and returned for the next troop lift, the enemy had Landing Zone X-Ray targeted. As Major Crandall and the first eight helicopters landed to discharge troops on his fifth troop lift, his unarmed helicopter came under such intense enemy fire that the ground commander ordered the second flight of eight aircraft to abort their mission. As Major Crandall flew back to Plei Me, his base of operations, he determined that the ground commander of the besieged infantry battalion desperately needed more ammunition. Major Crandall then decided to adjust his base of operations to Artillery Firebase Falcon in order to shorten the flight distance to deliver ammunition and evacuate wounded soldiers. While medical evacuation was not his mission, he immediately sought volunteers and with complete disregard for his own personal safety, led the two aircraft to Landing Zone X-Ray. Despite the fact that the landing zone was still under relentless enemy fire, Major Crandall landed and proceeded to supervise the loading of seriously wounded soldiers aboard his aircraft. Major Crandall's voluntary decision to land under the most extreme fire instilled in the other pilots the will and spirit to continue to land their own aircraft, and in the ground forces the realization that they would be resupplied and that friendly wounded would be promptly evacuated. This greatly enhanced morale and the will to fight at a critical time. After his first medical evacuation, Major Crandall continued to fly into and out of the landing zone throughout the day and into the evening. That day he completed a total of 22 flights, most under intense enemy fire, retiring from the battlefield only after all possible service had been rendered to the Infantry battalion. His actions provided critical resupply of ammunition and evacuation of the wounded. Major Crandall's daring acts of bravery and courage in the face of an overwhelming and determined enemy are in keeping with the highest traditions of the military service and reflect great credit upon himself, his unit, and the United States Army.

Duran, Jesus S.*

Specialist Duran's military records were reviewed under the FY2002 National Defense Authorization Act, P.L. 107-107, Section 552. P.L. 107-107 requested that the DOD review service records of certain Jewish Americans or Hispanic Americans who had been awarded the Distinguished Service Cross, Navy Cross, or Air Force Cross.

Rank and organization: Specialist Four, Company E, 2^d Battalion, 5th Cavalry, 1st Cavalry Division (Airmobile), U.S. Army. *Place and date:* Ph Romeas Hek, Cambodia, May 12, 1970. *Entered service at:* California. *Born:* July 26, 1948, Juarez, Mexico. *Date of issue:* March 18, 2014.

Citation: For conspicuous gallantry and intrepidity at the risk of his life above and beyond the call of duty:

Specialist Four Jesus S. Duran distinguished himself by acts of gallantry and intrepidity above and beyond the call of duty while serving as an acting M-60 machinegunner in Company E, 2nd Battalion, 5th Cavalry, 1st Cavalry Division (Airmobile) during combat operations against an armed enemy in the Republic of Vietnam on April 10, 1969. That afternoon, the reconnaissance platoon was moving into an elaborate enemy bunker complex when the lead elements began taking concentrated ambush fire from every side. The command post was in imminent danger of being overrun. With an M-60 machinegun blazing from his hip, Specialist Four Duran rushed forward and assumed a defensive position near the command post. As hostile forces stormed forward, Specialist Four Duran stood tall in a cloud of dust raised by the impacting rounds and bursting grenades directed toward him and thwarted the enemy with devastating streams of machinegun fire. Learning that two seriously wounded troopers lay helplessly pinned down under harassing fire, Specialist Four Duran assaulted the suppressive enemy positions, firing deadly bursts on the run. Mounting a log, he fired directly into the enemy's foxholes, eliminating four and cutting down several others as they fled. Specialist Four Duran then continued to pour effective fire on the disorganized and fleeing enemy. Specialist Four Duran's extraordinary heroism and selflessness above and beyond the call of duty are in keeping with the highest traditions of military service and reflect great credit upon himself, his unit, and the United States Army.

Erevia, Santiago J.

Rank and organization: Specialist Four, Company C, 1st Battalion, 501st Infantry, 101st Airborne Division, U.S. Army. *Place and date:* Tam Ky, Republic of Vietnam, May 21, 1969. *Entered service at:* San Antonio, TX. *Born:* 1946, Nordheim, TX. *Date of issue:* March 18, 2014.

Citation: For conspicuous gallantry and intrepidity at the risk of his life above and beyond the call of duty:

Specialist Four Santiago J. Erevia distinguished himself by acts of gallantry and intrepidity above and beyond the call of duty while serving as a radio telephone operator in Company C, 1st Battalion (Airmobile), 501st Infantry, 101st Airborne Division (Airmobile) during search-and-clear mission near Tam Ky, Republic of Vietnam on May 21, 1969. After breaching an insurgent perimeter, Specialist Four Erevia was designated by his platoon leader to render first aid to several casualties, and the rest of the platoon moved forward. As he was doing so, he came under intense hostile fire from four bunkers to his left front. Although he could have taken cover with the rest of the element, he chose a retaliatory course of action. With heavy enemy fire directed at him, he moved in full view of the hostile gunners as he proceeded to crawl from one wounded man to another, gathering ammunition. Armed with two M-16 rifles and several hand grenades, he charged toward the enemy positions behind the suppressive fire of the two rifles. Under very intense fire, he continued to advance on the insurgents until he was near the first bunker. Disregarding the enemy fire, he pulled the pin from a hand grenade and advanced on the bunker, leveling suppressive fire until he could drop the grenade into the bunker, mortally wounding the insurgent and destroying the fortification. Without hesitation, he employed identical tactics as he proceeded to eliminate the next two enemy positions. With the destruction of the third bunker, Specialist Four Erevia had exhausted his supply of hand grenades. Still under intense fire from the fourth position, he courageously charged forward behind the fire emitted by his M-16 rifles. Arriving at the very edge of the bunker, he silenced the occupant within the fortification at point-blank range. Through his heroic actions the lives of the wounded were saved and the members of the company command post were relieved from a very precarious situation. His exemplary performance in the face of overwhelming danger was an inspiration to his entire company and contributed immeasurably to the success of the mission. Specialist Four Erevia's conspicuous gallantry, extraordinary heroism, and intrepidity at the risk of his own life, above and beyond the call of duty, were in keeping with the highest traditions of military service and reflect great credit upon himself, his unit, and the United States Army.

Etchberger, Richard L.*

Rank and Organization: Chief Master Sergeant, Detachment 1, 1043rd Radar Evaluation Squadron, U.S. Air Force. *Place and date:* Phou Pha Thi, Laos, March 11, 1968. *Entered service at:* Harrisburg, PA. *Born:* March 5, 1933. *Place of birth:* unknown. *Date of issue:* September 21, 2010.

Citation: For conspicuous gallantry and intrepidity in action at the risk of his life above and beyond the call of duty.

Chief Etchberger and his team of technicians were manning a top secret defensive position at Lima Site 85 when the base was overrun by an enemy ground force. Receiving sustained and withering heavy artillery attacks directly upon his unit's position, Chief Etchberger's entire crew lay dead or severely wounded. Despite having received little or no combat training, Chief

Etchberger single-handedly held off the enemy with an M-16, while simultaneously directing air strikes into the area and calling for air rescue. Because of his fierce defense and heroic and selfless actions, he was able to deny the enemy access to his position and save the lives of his remaining crew. With the arrival of the rescue aircraft, Chief Etchberger, without hesitation, repeatedly and deliberately risked his own life, exposing himself to heavy enemy fire in order to place three surviving wounded comrades into rescue slings hanging from the hovering helicopter waiting to airlift them to safety. With his remaining crew safely aboard, Chief Etchberger finally climbed into an evacuation sling himself, only to be fatally wounded by enemy ground fire as he was being raised into the aircraft. Chief Etchberger's bravery and determination in the face of persistent enemy fire and overwhelming odds are in keeping with the highest standards of performance and traditions of military service. Chief Etchberger's gallantry, self-sacrifice, and profound concern for his fellow men at risk of his life, above and beyond the call of duty, reflect the highest credit upon himself and the United States Air Force.

Freeman, Ed W.

Congress approved a bill authorizing the award of the MOH to Corporal Smith and others on June 20, 2000, removing the statutory time limit on the award.

Rank and organization: Captain, 229th Assault Helicopter Battalion, 1st Cavalry Division (Airmobile), U.S. Army. *Place and date:* Ia Drang Valley, Republic of Vietnam. *Entered service at:* Hattiesburg, MS, September 13, 1948. *Born:* November 20, 1927, Neely, MS. *Date of issue:* July 16, 2001.

Citation: For conspicuous gallantry and intrepidity at the risk of his life above and beyond the call of duty.

Captain Ed W. Freeman, United States Army, distinguished himself by numerous acts of conspicuous gallantry and extraordinary intrepidity on 14 November 1965 while serving with Company A, 229th Assault Helicopter Battalion, 1st Cavalry Division (Airmobile). As a flight leader and second in command of a 16-helicopter lift unit, he supported a heavily engaged American infantry battalion at Landing Zone X-Ray in the Ia Drang Valley, Republic of Vietnam. The unit was almost out of ammunition after taking some of the heaviest casualties of the war, fighting off a relentless attack from a highly motivated, heavily armed enemy force. When the infantry commander closed the helicopter landing zone due to intense direct enemy fire, Captain Freeman risked his own life by flying his unarmed helicopter through a gauntlet of enemy fire time after time, delivering critically needed ammunition, water and medical supplies to the besieged battalion. His flights had a direct impact on the battle's outcome by providing the engaged units with timely supplies of ammunition critical to their survival, without which they would almost surely have gone down, with much greater loss of life. After medical evacuation helicopters refused to fly into the area due to intense enemy fire, Captain Freeman flew 14 separate rescue missions, providing life-saving evacuation of an estimated 30 seriously wounded soldiers—some of whom would not have survived had he not acted. All flights were made into a small emergency landing zone within 100 to 200 meters of the defensive perimeter where heavily committed units were perilously holding off the attacking elements. Captain Freeman's selfless acts of great valor, extraordinary perseverance and intrepidity were far above and beyond the call of duty or mission and set a superb example of leadership and courage for all of his peers.

Captain Freeman's extraordinary heroism and devotion to duty are in keeping with the highest traditions of military service and reflect great credit upon himself, his unit and the United States Army.

Garcia, Candelario*

Sergeant Garcia's military records were reviewed under the FY2002 National Defense Authorization Act, P.L. 107-107, Section 552. P.L. 107-107 requested that the DOD review service records of certain Jewish Americans or Hispanic Americans who had been awarded the Distinguished Service Cross, Navy Cross, or Air Force Cross.

Rank and organization: Sergeant, Company B, 1st Battalion, 2^d Infantry, 1st Brigade, 1st Infantry Division, U.S. Army. *Place and date:* Lai Khe, Republic of Vietnam, December 8, 1968. *Born:* February 26, 1944, Corsicana, TX. *Date of issue:* March 18, 2014.

Citation: For conspicuous gallantry and intrepidity at the risk of his life above and beyond the call of duty:

Sergeant Candelario Garcia distinguished himself by acts of gallantry and intrepidity above and beyond the call of duty while serving as an acting team leader for Company B, 1st Battalion, 2nd Infantry, 1st Brigade, 1st Infantry Division during combat operations against an armed enemy in Lai Khe, Republic of Vietnam, on December 8, 1968. On that day, while conducting reconnaissance, Sergeant Garcia and his platoon discovered communication wire and other signs of an enemy base camp leading into a densely vegetated area. As the men advanced, they came under intense fire. Several men were hit and trapped in the open. Ignoring a hail of hostile bullets, Sergeant Garcia crawled to within 10 meters of a machinegun bunker, leaped to his feet, and ran directly at the fortification, firing his rifle as he charged. Sergeant Garcia jammed two hand grenades into the gun port and then placed the muzzle of his weapon inside, killing all four occupants. Continuing to expose himself to intense enemy fire, Sergeant Garcia raced 15 meters to another bunker and killed its three defenders with hand grenades and rifle fire. After again braving the enemies' barrage in order to rescue two casualties, he joined his company in an assault that overran the remaining enemy positions. Sergeant Garcia's extraordinary heroism and selflessness above and beyond the call of duty are in keeping with the highest traditions of military service and reflect great credit upon himself, his unit, and the United States Army.

Ingram, Robert R.

Congress approved P.L. 105-103, November 20, 1997, removing the statutory time limit on the award for Petty Officer Ingram.

Rank and organization: Hospital Corpsman Third Class, U.S. Navy, serving with Company C, First Battalion, Seventh Marines, 1st Marine Division. *Place and date:* Ngai Province, Republic of Vietnam, 28 March 1966. *Entered service at:* Jacksonville, FL, September 30, 1963. *Born:* January 10, 1945, Clearwater, FL. *Date of issue:* July 10, 1998.

Citation: For conspicuous gallantry and intrepidity at the risk of his life above and beyond the call of duty while serving as Corpsman with Company C, First Battalion, Seventh Marines, against elements of a North Vietnam Aggressor (NVA) battalion in Quang Ngai Province, Republic of Vietnam on March 28, 1966.

Petty Officer Ingram accompanied the point platoon as it aggressively engaged an outpost of an NVA battalion. As the battle moved off a ridge line, down a tree-covered slope, to a small rice paddy and a village beyond, a tree line suddenly exploded with an intense hail of automatic rifle fire from approximately 100 North Vietnamese regulars. In moments, the platoon was decimated. Oblivious to the danger, Petty Officer Ingram crawled across the battlefield to reach a downed Marine. As he administered aid, a bullet went through the palm of his hand. Calls for "corpsmen" echoed across the ridge. Bleeding, he edged across the fire-swept landscape, collecting ammunition from the dead and administering aid to the wounded. Receiving two more wounds, with the third wound being a life-threatening one, he looked for a way off the face of the ridge, but again he heard the call for help and again he resolutely answered. He gathered magazines, resupplied and encouraged those capable of returning fire, and rendered aid to the more severely wounded until he finally reached the right flank of the platoon. While dressing the head wound of another corpsman, he sustained his fourth bullet wound. From 1600 hours until almost sunset, Petty Officer Ingram pushed, pulled, cajoled, and doctored his Marines. Enduring the pain from his many wounds and disregarding the probability of his own death, Petty Officer Ingram's gallant actions saved many lives. By his indomitable fighting spirit, daring initiative, and unfaltering dedication to duty, Petty Officer Ingram reflected great credit upon himself and upheld the highest traditions of the United States Naval Service.

Morris, Melvin

Rank and organization: Staff Sergeant Class, 3rd Company, 5th Special Forces Group (Airborne), 1st Special Forces, U.S. Army. *Place and date:* Chi Lang, Republic of Vietnam, September 17, 1969. *Entered service at:* Fort Bragg, NC. *Born:* January 7, 1942, Okmulgee, OK. *Date of issue:* March 18, 2014.

For conspicuous gallantry and intrepidity at the risk of his life above and beyond the call of duty:

Staff Sergeant Melvin Morris distinguished himself by acts of gallantry and intrepidity above and beyond the call of duty while serving as commander of a strike force drawn from Company D, 5th Special Forces Group (Airborne), 1st Special Forces, during combat operations against an armed enemy in the vicinity of Chi Lang, Republic of Vietnam, on September 17, 1969. On that afternoon, Staff Sergeant Morris's affiliated companies encountered an extensive enemy mine field and were subsequently engaged by a hostile force. Staff Sergeant Morris learned by radio that a fellow team commander had been killed near an enemy bunker and he immediately reorganized his men into an effective assault posture before advancing forward and splitting off with two men to recover the team commander's body. Observing the maneuver, the hostile force concentrated its fire on Staff Sergeant Morris's three-man element and successfully wounded both men accompanying him. After assisting the two wounded men back to his forces' lines, Staff Sergeant Morris charged forward into withering enemy fire with only his men's suppressive fire as cover. While enemy machine gun emplacements continuously directed strafing fusillades against him, Staff Sergeant Morris destroyed the positions with hand grenades and continued his assault, ultimately eliminating four bunkers. Upon reaching the bunker nearest the fallen team commander, Staff Sergeant Morris repulsed the enemy, retrieved his comrade and began the arduous trek back to friendly lines. He was wounded three times as he struggled forward, but ultimately succeeded in returning his fallen comrade to a friendly position. Staff Sergeant Morris's extraordinary heroism and selflessness above and beyond the call of duty are in keeping with the highest traditions of military service and reflect great credit upon himself, his unit, and the United States Army.

Pitsenbarger, William H.*

Congress approved the FY2001 National Defense Authorization Act, P.L. 106-398, Section 548, removing the statutory time limit on the award for Airman First Class Pitsenbarger.

Rank and organization: Airman First Class, Pararescue Crew Member, Detachment 6, 38th Aerospace Rescue and Recovery Squadron, U.S. Air Force. *Place and date:* Near Cam My, Republic of Vietnam. *Entered service at:* Piqua, OH, December 31, 1962. *Born:* July 8, 1944, Piqua, OH. *Date of issue:* December 8, 2000.

Citation: For conspicuous gallantry and intrepidity at the risk of his life above and beyond the call of duty.

Airman First Class Pitsenbarger distinguished himself by extreme valor on 11 April 1966 near Cam My, Republic of Vietnam, while assigned as a Pararescue Crew Member, Detachment 6, 38th Aerospace Rescue and Recovery Squadron. On that date, Airman Pitsenbarger was aboard a rescue helicopter responding to a call for evacuation of casualties incurred in an ongoing firefight between elements of the United States Army's 1st Infantry Division and a sizeable enemy force approximately 35 miles east of Saigon. With complete disregard for personal safety, Airman Pitsenbarger volunteered to ride a hoist more than one hundred feet through the jungle, to the ground. On the ground, he organized and coordinated rescue efforts, cared for the wounded, prepared casualties for evacuation, and insured that the recovery operation continued in a smooth and orderly fashion. Through his personal efforts, the evacuation of the wounded was greatly expedited. As each of the nine casualties evacuated that day was recovered, Airman Pitsenbarger refused evacuation in order to get more wounded soldiers to safety. After several pick-ups, one of the two rescue helicopters involved in the evacuation was struck by heavy enemy ground fire and was forced to leave the scene for an emergency landing. Airman Pitsenbarger stayed behind on the ground to perform medical duties. Shortly thereafter, the area came under sniper and mortar fire. During a subsequent attempt to evacuate the site, American forces came under heavy assault by a large Viet Cong force. When the enemy launched the assault, the evacuation was called off and Airman Pitsenbarger took up arms with the besieged infantrymen. He courageously resisted the enemy, braving intense gunfire to gather and distribute vital ammunition to American defenders. As the battle raged on, he repeatedly exposed himself to enemy fire to care for the wounded, pull them out of the line of fire, and return fire whenever he could, during which time he was wounded three times. Despite his wounds, he valiantly fought on, simultaneously treating as many wounded as possible. In the vicious fighting that followed, the American forces suffered 80% casualties as their perimeter was breached, and Airman Pitsenbarger was fatally wounded. Airman Pitsenbarger exposed himself to almost certain death by staying on the ground, and perished while saving the lives of wounded infantrymen.

His bravery and determination exemplify the highest professional standards and traditions of military service and reflect great credit upon himself, his unit, and the United States Air Force.

Rascon, Alfred

Congress approved P.L. 106-65 on October 5, 1999, removing the statutory time limit on the award for Specialist Four Rascon.

Rank and organization: Specialist Four, U.S. Army, Reconnaissance Platoon, Headquarters Company, First Battalion (Airborne), 503rd Infantry, 173rd Airborne Brigade (Separate). *Place and date:* Long Khanh Province, Republic of Vietnam, March 16, 1966. *Entered service at:* Fort Ord, CA, August 1963. *Born:* September 10, 1945, Chihuahua, Mexico. *Date of issue:* February 8, 2000.

Citation: Specialist Four Alfred Rascon distinguished himself by a series of extraordinarily courageous acts on March 16, 1966, while assigned as a medic to the Reconnaissance Platoon, Headquarters Company First Battalion (Airborne), 503rd Infantry, 173rd Airborne Brigade (Separate).

While moving to reinforce its sister battalion under intense enemy attack, the reconnaissance platoon came under heavy fire from a numerically superior enemy force. The intense fire from crew-served weapons and grenades severely wounded several point squad soldiers. Specialist Four Rascon, ignoring directions to stay behind shelter until cover fire could be provided, made his way forward. He repeatedly tried to reach the severely wounded point machine-gunner lying on an open enemy trail, but was driven back each time by withering fire. Finally, he jumped to his feet and, with total disregard for his personal safety, he raced through heavy enemy fire and exploding grenades to reach his wounded comrade. He then intentionally placed his body between the soldier and the enemy machine guns, sustaining numerous shrapnel injuries and a serious wound to the hip. Ignoring his own wounds, he dragged the larger soldier from the fire-raked trail. Hearing a second machine gunner yell that he was running out of ammunition, Specialist Four Rascon, still under heavy enemy fire, crawled back to the wounded machine-gunner, stripped him of his bandoleers of ammunition, and gave them to the machine gunner, who continued his suppressive fire. Later, Specialist Four Rascon, fearing the abandoned machine gun, its ammunition, and spare barrel should fall into enemy hands, made his way to retrieve them. On his way, he was wounded in the face and torso by grenade fragments, but continued to recover the abandoned machine gun, ammunition, and spare barrel items, enabling another soldier to provide added suppressive fire to the pinned-downed squad. While searching for additional wounded, he saw the point grenadier wounded by small arms fire and grenades. With complete disregard for his own life, Specialist Four Rascon covered the wounded soldier with his body, thereby absorbing the blasts from the exploding grenades and saving the soldier's life. As grenades were being thrown at the wounded point squad leader, Specialist Rascon again, in completed disregard for his own life, covered the soldier with his body, absorbing the full force of the grenade explosions. Once more, Specialist Four Rascon was critically wounded by shrapnel, but again he continued to search for and aid the wounded. Although severely wounded, he remained on the battlefield himself, and continued treating the wounded and directing their evacuation. Only after being placed on the evacuation helicopter did he allow aid to be given to himself.

Specialist Four Rascon's extraordinary valor in the face of deadly enemy fire, his heroism in rescuing the wounded, and his gallantry by repeatedly risking his own life for his fellow soldiers are in keeping with the highest traditions of the military service and reflect great credit upon himself, his unit, and the United States Army.

Rodela, Jose

Sergeant Rodela's military records were reviewed under the FY2002 National Defense Authorization Act, P.L. 107-107, Section 552. P.L. 107-107 requested that the DOD review service records of certain Jewish Americans or Hispanic Americans who had been awarded the Distinguished Service Cross, Navy Cross, or Air Force Cross.

Rank and organization: Sergeant First Class, Operational Detachment Alpha 3312, U.S. Army. *Place and date:* Phuoc Long Province, Republic of Vietnam, September 1, 1969. *Entered service at:* Corpus Christi, TX. *Born:* June 15, 1937, Corpus Christi, TX. *Date of issue:* March 18, 2014.

Citation: For conspicuous gallantry and intrepidity at the risk of his life above and beyond the call of duty:

Sergeant First Class Jose Rodela distinguished himself by acts of gallantry and intrepidity above and beyond the call of duty while serving as the company commander, Detachment B-36, Company A, 5th Special Forces Group (Airborne), 1st Special Forces during combat operations against an armed enemy in Phuoc Long Province, Republic of Vietnam, on September 1, 1969. That afternoon, Sergeant First Class Rodela's battalion came under an intense barrage of mortar, rocket, and machinegun fire. Ignoring the withering enemy fire, Sergeant First Class Rodela immediately began placing his men into defensive positions to prevent the enemy from overrunning the entire battalion. Repeatedly exposing himself to enemy fire, Sergeant First Class Rodela moved from position to position, providing suppressing fire and assisting wounded, and was himself wounded in the back and head by a B-40 rocket while recovering a wounded comrade. Alone, Sergeant First Class Rodela assaulted and knocked out the B-40 rocket position before successfully returning to the battalion's perimeter. Sergeant First Class Rodela's extraordinary heroism and selflessness above and beyond the call of duty are in keeping with the highest traditions of military service and reflect great credit upon himself, his unit, and the United States Army.

Sabo, Jr. Leslie H.*

Specialist-Four Class Sabo's original nomination for the MOH was lost in 1970. It was discovered by a researcher at the National Archives in 1999.[19] H.R. 1585, which became P.L. 110-181, authorized and requested that the President award the MOH posthumously to Specialist Sabo. The law also provides that in such cases time limitations may be waived.[20]

Rank and organization: Specialist Fourth Class, Company B, 3rd Battalion, 506th Infantry, 101st Airborne Division, U.S. Army. *Place and date:* Se San, Cambodia, May 10, 1970. *Entered service at:* Ellwood City, PA. *Born:* February 23, 1948, Austria. *Date of issue:* May 16, 2012.

Citation: Specialist-Four Leslie H. Sabo Jr. distinguished himself by conspicuous acts of gallantry and intrepidity above and beyond the call of duty at the cost of his own life while serving as a rifleman in Company B, 3rd Battalion, 506th Infantry, 101st Airborne Division in Se San, Cambodia, on May 10, 1970.

On that day, Specialist-Four Sabo and his platoon were conducting a reconnaissance patrol when they were ambushed from all sides by a large enemy force. Without hesitation, Specialist-Four Sabo charged an enemy position, killing several enemy soldiers. Immediately thereafter, he assaulted an enemy flanking force, successfully drawing their fire away from friendly soldiers and ultimately forcing the enemy to retreat. In order to re-supply ammunition, he sprinted across an open field to a wounded comrade. As he began to reload, an enemy grenade landed nearby. Specialist-Four Sabo picked it up, threw it, and shielded his comrade with his own body, thus absorbing the brunt of the blast and saving his comrade's life. Seriously wounded by the blast, Specialist Four Sabo nonetheless retained the initiative and then single-handedly charged an enemy bunker that had inflicted severe damage on the platoon, receiving several serious wounds from automatic weapons fire in the process. Now mortally injured, he crawled towards the enemy emplacement and, when in position, threw a grenade into the bunker. The resulting explosion silenced the enemy fire, but also ended Specialist-Four Sabo's life. His indomitable courage and complete disregard for his own safety saved the lives of many of his platoon members. Specialist-Four Sabo's extraordinary heroism and selflessness, above and beyond the call of duty, at the cost of his life, are in keeping with the highest traditions of military service and reflect great credit upon himself, Company B, 3rd Battalion, 506th Infantry, 101st Airborne Division, and the United States Army.

Sloat, Donald P.*

In H.R. 3304, the National Defense Authorization Act for Fiscal Year 2014, P.L. 113-66, Congress authorized the President of the United States to award the MOH to Specialist Sloat, waiving time limitations found in 10 U.S.C. § 3744.

---

[19] *Soldiers*, May 15, 2012, "Gallantry to Be Honored After 42 Years," at http://www.army mil/article/79892/.

[20] 10 U.S.C. Medal of Honor §3744.

Rank and organization: Specialist 4, Company D, 2nd Battalion, 1st Infantry Regiment, 196th Light Infantry Brigade, Americal Division, U.S. Army. *Place and date:* Hawk Hill Firebase, Republic of Vietnam, January 17, 1970. *Entered service at:* unknown. *Born:* unknown. *Date of issue:* September 15, 2014.

On the morning of January 17, 1970, Sloat's squad was conducting a patrol, serving as a blocking element in support of tanks and armored personnel carriers from F Troop in the Que Son valley. As the squad moved up a small hill in file formation, the lead soldier tripped a wire attached to a hand grenade booby trap set up by enemy forces. When the grenade rolled down the hill toward Sloat, he had a choice. He could hit the ground and seek cover or pick up the grenade and throw it away from his fellow soldiers. After initially attempting to throw the grenade, Sloat realized that detonation was imminent, and that two or three men near him would be killed or seriously injured if he couldn't shield them from the blast. In an instant, Sloat chose to draw the grenade to his body, shielding his squad members from the blast, and saving their lives. Sloat's actions define the ultimate sacrifice of laying down his own life in order to save the lives of his comrades. Specialist Four Donald P. Sloat's extraordinary heroism and selflessness are in keeping with the highest traditions of military service, and reflect great credit upon himself, his unit, and the United States Army.

Swanson, Jon E.*

Congress approved the FY2002 National Defense Authorization Act, P.L. 107-107, Section 551, on December 28, 2001, removing the statutory time limit on the award for Captain Swanson.

Rank and organization: Captain, Troop B, First Squadron, Ninth Cavalry, First Cavalry Division (Airmobile), U.S. Army. *Place and date:* Kingdom of Cambodia, 26 February 1971. *Entered service at:* Denver, CO. *Born:* May 1, 1942, San Antonio, TX. *Date of issue:* May 1, 2002.

Citation: For conspicuous gallantry and intrepidity at the risk of his life above and beyond the call of duty.

Captain Jon E. Swanson distinguished himself by acts of bravery on February 26, 1971, while flying an OH-6A aircraft in support of ARVN Task Force 333 in the Kingdom of Cambodia. With two well-equipped enemy regiments known to be in the area, Captain Swanson was tasked with pinpointing the enemy's precise positions. Captain Swanson flew at treetop level at a slow airspeed, making his aircraft a vulnerable target. The advancing ARVN unit came under heavy automatic weapons fire from enemy bunkers 100 meters to their front. Exposing his aircraft to enemy anti-aircraft fire, Captain Swanson immediately engaged the enemy bunkers with concussion grenades and machine gun fire. After destroying five bunkers and evading intense ground-to-air fire, he observed a .51 caliber machine gun position. With all his heavy ordnance expended on the bunkers, he did not have sufficient explosives to destroy the position. Consequently, he marked the position with a smoke grenade and directed a Cobra gun ship attack. After completion of the attack, Captain Swanson found the weapon still intact and an enemy soldier crawling over to man it. He immediately engaged the individual and killed him. During this time, his aircraft sustained several hits from another .51 caliber machine gun. Captain Swanson engaged the position with his aircraft's weapons, marked the target, and directed a second Cobra gun ship attack. He volunteered to continue the mission, despite the fact that he was now critically low on ammunition and his aircraft was crippled by enemy fire. As Captain Swanson attempted to fly toward another .51 caliber machine gun position, his aircraft exploded in the air and crashed to the ground, causing his death. Captain Swanson's courageous actions resulted in at least eight enemy killed and the destruction of three enemy anti-aircraft weapons.

Captain Swanson's extraordinary heroism and devotion to duty are in keeping with the highest traditions of military service and reflect great credit upon himself, his unit, and the United States Army.

The Unknown Soldier*

P.L. 98-301 authorized the President to award the Medal of Honor to the Unknown Soldier of the Vietnam War. The Medal was bestowed during interment ceremonies on Memorial Day, May 28, 1984. In June 1998, the Department of Defense announced that the results of DNA tests on the remains of the Vietnam Unknown confirmed his identity as Air Force First Lieutenant Michael J. Blassie. His remains were returned to his family and reinterred in St. Louis. Members of Blassie's family requested that he retain the Medal. The Pentagon denied this request, stating that the Vietnam Unknown Medal of Honor will be kept on permanent display at Arlington National Cemetery in symbolic tribute to all who lost their lives in the Vietnam War.

Versace, Humbert R.*

Congress approved the FY2002 National Defense Authorization Act, P.L. 107-107, Section 551, on December 28, 2001, removing the statutory time limit on the award for Captain Versace.

Rank and organization: Captain, Detachment A, 5th Special Forces Group, Special Operations Group, Military Assistance Command, U.S. Army. *Place and date:* Ca Mau, Republic of Vietnam. *Entered service at:* West Point, NY, June 3, 1959. *Born:* July 2, 1937, Honolulu, HI. *Date of issue:* July 8, 2002.

Citation: For conspicuous gallantry and intrepidity at the risk of his life above and beyond the call of duty.

Captain Humbert R. Versace distinguished himself by extraordinary heroism during the period of 29 October 1963 to 26 September 1965, while serving as S-2 Advisor, Military Assistance Advisory Group, Detachment 52, Ca Mau, Republic of Vietnam. While accompanying a Civilian Irregular Defense Group patrol engaged in combat operations in Thoi Binh District, An Xuyen Province, Captain Versace and the patrol came under sudden and intense mortar, automatic weapons, and small arms fire from elements of a heavily armed enemy battalion. As the battle raged, Captain Versace, although severely wounded in the knee and back by hostile fire, fought valiantly and continued to engage enemy targets. Weakened by his wounds and fatigued by the fierce firefight, Captain Versace stubbornly resisted capture by the over-powering Viet Cong force with the last full measure of his strength and ammunition. Taken prisoner by the Viet Cong, he exemplified the tenets of the Code of Conduct from the time he entered into Prisoner of War status. Captain Versace assumed command of his fellow American soldiers, scorned the enemy's exhaustive interrogation and indoctrination efforts, and made three unsuccessful attempts to escape, despite his weakened condition, which was brought about by his wounds and the extreme privation and hardships he was forced to endure. During his captivity, Captain Versace was segregated in an isolated prisoner of war cage, manacled in irons for prolonged periods of time, and placed on extremely reduced ration. The enemy was unable to break his indomitable will, his faith in God, and his trust in the United States of America. Captain Versace, an American fighting man who epitomized the principles of his country and the Code of Conduct, was executed by the Viet Cong on 26 September 1965.

Captain Versace's gallant actions in close contact with an enemy force and unyielding courage and bravery while a prisoner of war are in the highest traditions of the military service and reflect the utmost credit upon himself and the United States Army.

Somalia

Gordon, Gary I.*

Rank and organization: Master Sergeant, U.S. Army. *Place and date:* October 3,1993, Mogadishu, Somalia. *Entered service at:* unknown. *Born:* August 13, 1968, Lincoln, ME. *Date of issue:* May 23, 1994.

Citation: Master Sergeant Gordon, United States Army, distinguished himself by actions above and beyond the call of duty. On 3 October 1993, while serving as Sniper Team Leader, United States Army Special Operations Command with Task Force Ranger in Mogadishu, Somalia.

Master Sergeant Gordon's sniper team provided precision fire from the lead helicopter during an assault and at two helicopter crash sites, while subjected to intense automatic weapons and rocket propelled grenade fires. When Master Sergeant Gordon learned that ground forces were not immediately available to secure the second crash site, he and another sniper unhesitatingly volunteered to be inserted to protect four critically wounded personnel, despite being well aware of the growing number of enemy personnel closing in on the site. After his third request to be inserted, Master Sergeant Gordon received permission to perform his volunteer mission. When debris and enemy ground fires at the site caused them to abort the first attempt, Master Sergeant Gordon was inserted 100 meters south of the crash site. Equipped with only his sniper rifle and a pistol, Master Sergeant Gordon and his fellow sniper, while under intense small arms fire from the enemy, fought their way through a dense maze of shanties and shacks to reach the critically injured crew members. Master Sergeant Gordon immediately pulled the pilot and the other crew members from the aircraft, establishing a perimeter which placed him and his fellow sniper in the most vulnerable position. Master Sergeant Gordon used his long range rifle and side arm to kill an undetermined number of attackers until he depleted his ammunition. Master Sergeant Gordon then went back to the wreckage, recovering some of the crew's weapons and ammunition. Despite the fact that he was critically low on ammunition, he provided some of it to the dazed pilot and then radioed for help. Master Sergeant Gordon continued to travel the perimeter, protecting the downed crew. After his team member was fatally wounded and his own rifle ammunition exhausted, Master Sergeant Gordon returned to the wreckage, recovered a rifle with the last five rounds of ammunition and gave it to the pilot with the words, "good luck." Then, armed only with his pistol, Master Sergeant Gordon continued to fight until he was fatally wounded. His actions saved the pilot's life.

Master Sergeant Gordon's extraordinary heroism and devotion to duty were in keeping with the highest standards of military service and reflect great credit upon him, his unit, and the United States Army.

Shughart, Randall D.*

Rank and organization: Sergeant First Class, U.S. Army. *Place and date:* 3 October 1993, Mogadishu, Somalia. *Entered service at:* unknown. *Born:* August 30, 1960, Lincoln, NE. *Date of issue:* May 24, 1994.

Citation: Sergeant First Class Shughart, United States Army, distinguished himself by actions above and beyond the call of duty. On October 1993, while serving as a Sniper Team Member, United States Army Special Operations Command with Task Force Ranger in Mogadishu, Somalia.

Sergeant First Class Shughart provided precision sniper fire from the lead helicopter during an assault on a building and at two helicopter crash sites, while subjected to intense automatic weapons and rocket propelled grenade fire. While providing critical suppressive fire at the second crash site, Sergeant First Class Shughart and his team leader learned that ground forces were not immediately available to secure the site. Sergeant First Class Shughart and his team leader unhesitatingly volunteered to be inserted to protect the four critically wounded personnel, despite being well aware of the growing number of enemy personnel closing in on the site. After their third request to be inserted, Sergeant First Class Shughart and his team leader received permission to perform this volunteer mission. When debris and enemy ground fires at the site caused them to abort the first attempt, Sergeant First Class Shughart and his team leader were inserted 100 meters south of the crash site. Equipped with only his sniper rifle and a pistol, Sergeant First Class Shughart and his team leader, while under intense small arms fire from the enemy, fought their way through a dense maze of shanties and shacks to reach the critically injured crew members. Sergeant First Class Shughart pulled the pilot and the other crew members from the aircraft, establishing a perimeter which placed him and his fellow sniper in the most vulnerable position. Sergeant First Class Shughart used his long range rifle and side arm to kill an undetermined number of attackers while traveling the perimeter, protecting the downed crew. Sergeant First Class Shughart continued his protective fire until he depleted his ammunition and was fatally wounded. His actions saved the pilot's life.

Sergeant First Class Shughart's extraordinary heroism and devotion to duty were in keeping with the highest standards of military service and reflect great credit upon him, his unit, and the United States Army.

Afghanistan

Carpenter, William Kyle

Rank and organization: Lance Corporal, Company F, 2nd Battalion, 9th Marines, Regimental Combat Team 1, 1st Marine Division (Forward), 1st Marine Expeditionary Force (Forward). *Place and date:* Marjah District, Helmand Province, Afghanistan, November 21, 2010. *Entered service at:* Columbia, SC. *Born:* October 17, 1989, Flowood, MS. *Date of issue:* June 19, 2014.

Citation: For conspicuous gallantry and intrepidity at the risk of his life above and beyond the call of duty while serving as an Automatic Rifleman with Company F, 2nd Battalion, 9th Marines, Regimental Combat Team 1, 1st Marine Division (Forward), 1 Marine Expeditionary Force (Forward), in Helmand Province, Afghanistan, in support of Operation Enduring Freedom on November 21, 2010. Lance Corporal Carpenter was a member of a platoon-size coalition force, comprised of two reinforced Marine squads partnered with an Afghan National Army squad. The platoon had established Patrol Base Dakota two days earlier in a small village in the Marjah District in order to disrupt enemy activity and provide security for the local Afghan population. Lance Corporal Carpenter and a fellow Marine were manning a rooftop security position on the perimeter of Patrol Base Dakota when the enemy initiated a daylight attack with hand grenades, one of which landed inside their sandbagged position. Without hesitation, and with complete disregard for his own safety, Lance Corporal Carpenter moved toward the grenade in an attempt to shield his fellow Marine from the deadly blast. When the grenade detonated, his body absorbed the brunt of the blast, severely wounding him, but saving the life of his fellow Marine. By his undaunted courage, bold fighting spirit, and unwavering devotion to duty in the face of almost certain death, Lance Corporal Carpenter reflected great credit upon himself and upheld the highest traditions of the Marine Corps and the United States Naval Service.

Carter, Ty M.

Rank and organization: Specialist, B Troop, 3rd Squadron, 61st Cavalry Regiment, U.S. Army. *Place and date:* Outpost Keating, Nuristan Province, Afghanistan, October 3, 2009. *Entered service at:* Antioch, CA. *Born:* January 25, 1980, Spokane, WA. *Date of issue:* August 26, 2013.

Citation: For conspicuous gallantry and intrepidity at the risk of his life above and beyond the call of duty: Specialist Ty M. Carter distinguished himself by acts of gallantry and intrepidity at the risk of his life above and beyond the call of duty while serving as a Scout with Bravo Troop, 3d Squadron, 61st Cavalry Regiment, 4th Brigade Combat Team, 4th Infantry Division, during combat operations against an armed enemy in Kamdesh District, Nuristan Province, Afghanistan on October 3, 2009.

On that morning, Specialist Carter and his comrades awakened to an attack of an estimated 300 enemy fighters occupying the high ground on all four sides of Combat Outpost Keating, employing concentrated fire from recoilless rifles, rocket propelled grenades, anti-aircraft machine guns, mortars and small arms fire. Specialist Carter reinforced a forward battle position, ran twice through a 100 meter gauntlet of enemy fire to resupply ammunition and voluntarily remained there to defend the isolated position. Armed with only an M4 carbine rifle, Specialist Carter placed accurate, deadly fire on the enemy, beating back the assault force and preventing the position from being overrun, over the course of several hours. With complete disregard for his own safety and in spite of his own wounds, he ran through a hail of enemy rocket propelled grenade and machine gun fire to rescue a critically wounded comrade who had been pinned down in an exposed position. Specialist Carter rendered life extending first aid and carried the Soldier to cover. On his own initiative, Specialist Carter again maneuvered through enemy fire to check on a fallen Soldier and recovered the squad's radio, which allowed them to coordinate their evacuation with fellow Soldiers. With teammates providing covering fire, Specialist Carter assisted in moving the wounded Soldier 100 meters through withering enemy fire to the aid station and before returning to the fight. Specialist Carter's heroic actions and tactical skill were critical to the defense of Combat Outpost Keating, preventing the enemy from capturing the position and saving the lives of his fellow Soldiers. Specialist Ty M. Carter's extraordinary heroism and selflessness above and beyond the call of duty are in keeping with the highest traditions of military service and reflect great credit upon himself, Bravo Troop, 3d Squadron, 61st Cavalry Regiment, 4th Brigade Combat Team, 4th Infantry Division and the United States Army.

Giunta, Salvatore A.

Rank and organization: Staff Sergeant, Battle Company, Company B, 2nd Battalion (Airborne), 503rd Infantry Regiment, U.S. Army. *Place and date:* Korengal Valley, Afghanistan, October 25, 2007. *Entered service at:* Cedar Rapids, IA. *Born:* January 21, 1985, Clinton, IA. *Date of issue:* November 16, 2010.

Citation: Specialist Salvatore A. Giunta distinguished himself conspicuously by gallantry and intrepidity at the risk of his life above and beyond the call of duty in action with an armed enemy in the Korengal Valley, Afghanistan, on October 25, 2007.

While conducting a patrol as team leader with Company B, 2nd Battalion (Airborne), 503rd Infantry Regiment, Specialist Giunta and his team were navigating through harsh terrain when they were ambushed by a well-armed and well-coordinated insurgent force. While under heavy enemy fire, Specialist Giunta immediately sprinted towards cover and engaged the enemy. Seeing that his squad leader had fallen and believing that he had been injured, Specialist Giunta exposed himself to withering enemy fire and raced towards his squad leader, helped him to cover, and administered medical aid. While administering first aid, enemy fire struck Specialist Giunta's body armor and his secondary weapon. Without regard to the ongoing fire, Specialist Giunta engaged the enemy before prepping and throwing grenades, using the explosions for cover in order to conceal his position. Attempting to reach additional wounded fellow soldiers who were separated from the squad, Specialist Giunta and his team encountered a barrage of enemy fire that forced them to the ground. The team continued forward and upon reaching the wounded soldiers, Specialist Giunta realized that another soldier was still separated from the element. Specialist Giunta then advanced forward on his own initiative. As he crested the top of a hill, he observed two insurgents carrying away an American soldier. He immediately engaged the enemy, killing one and wounding the other. Upon reaching the wounded soldier, he began to provide medical aid, as his squad caught up and provided security. Specialist Giunta's unwavering courage, selflessness, and decisive leadership while under extreme enemy fire were integral to his platoon's ability to defeat an enemy ambush and recover a fellow American soldier from the enemy. Specialist Salvatore A. Giunta's extraordinary heroism and selflessness above and beyond the call of duty are in keeping with the highest traditions of military service and reflect great credit upon himself, Company B, 2nd Battalion (Airborne), 503rd Infantry Regiment, and the United States Army.

Meyer, Dakota

Rank and organization: Sergeant, Embedded Training Team 2-8, Regional Corps Advisory Command 3-7, U.S. Marine Corps. *Place and date:* Kunar Province, Afghanistan, September 8, 2009. *Entered service at:* Louisville, KY. *Born:* June 26, 1988, Louisville, KY. *Date of issue:* September 15, 2011.

Citation: Corporal Meyer maintained security at a patrol rally point while other members of his team moved on foot with two platoons of Afghan National Army and Border Police into the village of Ganjgal for a pre-dawn meeting with village elders.

Moving into the village, the patrol was ambushed by more than 50 enemy fighters firing rocket propelled grenades, mortars, and machine guns from houses and fortified positions on the slopes above. Hearing over the radio that four U.S. team members were cut off, Corporal Meyer seized the initiative. With a fellow Marine driving, Corporal Meyer took the exposed gunner's position in a gun-truck as they drove down the steeply terraced terrain in a daring attempt to disrupt the enemy attack and locate the trapped U.S. team. Disregarding intense enemy fire now concentrated on their lone vehicle, Corporal Meyer killed a number of enemy fighters with the mounted machine guns and his rifle, some at near point blank range, as he and his driver made three solo trips into the ambush area. During the first two trips, he and his driver evacuated two dozen Afghan soldiers, many of whom were wounded. When one machine gun became inoperable, he directed a return to the rally point to switch to another gun-truck for a third trip into the ambush area where his accurate fire directly supported the remaining U.S. personnel and Afghan soldiers fighting their way out of the ambush. Despite a shrapnel wound to his arm, Corporal Meyer made two more trips into the ambush area in a third gun-truck accompanied by four other Afghan vehicles to recover more wounded Afghan soldiers and search for the missing U.S. team members. Still under heavy enemy fire, he dismounted the vehicle on the fifth trip and moved on foot to locate and recover the bodies of his team members. Corporal Meyer's daring initiative and bold fighting spirit throughout the 6-hour battle significantly disrupted the enemy's attack and inspired the members of the combined force to fight on. His unwavering courage and steadfast devotion to his U.S. and Afghan comrades in the face of almost certain death reflected great credit upon himself and upheld the highest traditions of the Marine Corps and the United States Naval Service.

Miller, Robert J.*

Rank and organization: Staff Sergeant, Special Forces Operational Detachment Alpha 3312, Special Operations Task Force 33, U.S. Army. *Place and date:* Gowardesh Valley, Konar Province, Afghanistan, January 25, 2008. *Entered service at:* Oviedo, FL. *Born:* October 14, 1983. *Place of Birth:* unknown. *Date of issue:* October 6, 2010.

Citation: Robert J. Miller distinguished himself by extraordinary acts of heroism while serving as the Weapons Sergeant in Special Forces Operational Detachment Alpha 3312, Special Operations Task Force-33, Combined Joint Special Operations Task Force-Afghanistan during combat operations against an armed enemy in Konar Province, Afghanistan on January 25, 2008.

While conducting a combat reconnaissance patrol through the Gowardesh Valley, Staff Sergeant Miller and his small element of U.S. and Afghan National Army soldiers engaged a force of 15 to 20 insurgents occupying prepared fighting positions. Staff Sergeant Miller initiated the assault by engaging the enemy positions with his vehicle's turret-mounted Mark-19 40 millimeter automatic grenade launcher while simultaneously providing detailed descriptions of the enemy positions to his command, enabling effective, accurate close air support. Following the engagement, Staff Sergeant Miller led a small squad forward to conduct a battle damage assessment. As the group neared the small, steep, narrow valley that the enemy had inhabited, a large, well-coordinated insurgent force initiated a near ambush, assaulting from elevated positions with ample cover. Exposed and with little available cover, the patrol was totally vulnerable to enemy rocket propelled grenades and automatic weapon fire. As point man, Staff Sergeant Miller was at the front of the patrol, cut off from supporting elements, and less than 20 meters from enemy forces. Nonetheless, with total disregard for his own safety, he called for his men to quickly move back to covered positions as he charged the enemy over exposed ground and under overwhelming enemy fire in order to provide protective fire for his team. While maneuvering to engage the enemy, Staff Sergeant Miller was shot in his upper torso. Ignoring the wound, he continued to push the fight, moving to draw fire from over one hundred enemy fighters upon himself. He then again charged forward through an open area in order to allow his teammates to safely reach cover. After killing at least 10 insurgents, wounding dozens more, and repeatedly exposing himself to withering enemy fire while moving from position to position, Staff Sergeant Miller was mortally wounded by enemy fire. His extraordinary valor ultimately saved the lives of seven members of his own team and 15 Afghanistan National Army soldiers. Staff Sergeant Miller's heroism and selflessness above and beyond the call of duty, and at the cost of his own life, are in keeping with the highest traditions of military service and reflect great credit upon himself and the United States Army.

Monti, Jared C.*

Rank and organization: Sergeant First Class, U.S. Army, Headquarters Company, 10th Mountain Division U.S. Army. *Place and date:* Nuristan Province, Afghanistan, June 21, 2006. *Entered service at:* Rayntham, MA. *Born:* September 20, 1975, Abington, MA. *Date of issue:* September 17, 2009.

Citation: Staff Sergeant Jared C. Monti distinguished himself by acts of gallantry and intrepidity above and beyond the call of duty while serving as a team leader with Headquarters and Headquarters Troop, 3rd Squadron, 71st Cavalry Regiment, 3rd Brigade Combat Team, 10th Mountain Division, in connection with combat operations against an armed enemy in Nuristan Province, Afghanistan, on June 21, 2006.

While Staff Sergeant Monti was leading a mission aimed at gathering intelligence and directing fire against the enemy, his 16-man patrol was attacked by as many as 50 enemy fighters. On the verge of being overrun, Staff Sergeant Monti quickly directed his men to set up a defensive position behind a rock formation. He then called for indirect fire support, accurately targeting the rounds upon the enemy who had closed to within 50 meters of his position. While still directing fire, Staff Sergeant Monti personally engaged the enemy with his rifle and a grenade, successfully disrupting an attempt to flank his patrol. Staff Sergeant Monti then realized that one of his Soldiers was lying wounded in the open ground between the advancing enemy and the patrol's position. With complete disregard for his own safety, Staff Sergeant Monti twice attempted to move from behind the cover of the rocks into the face of relentless enemy fire to rescue his fallen comrade. Determined not to leave his Soldier, Staff Sergeant Monti made a third attempt to cross open terrain through intense enemy fire. On this final attempt, he was mortally wounded, sacrificing his own life in an effort to save his fellow Soldier. Staff Sergeant Monti's selfless acts of heroism inspired his patrol to fight off the larger enemy force. Staff Sergeant Monti's immeasurable courage and uncommon valor are in keeping with the highest traditions of military service and reflect great credit upon himself, Headquarters and Headquarters Troop, 3rd Squadron, 71st Cavalry Regiment, 3rd Brigade Combat Team, 10th Mountain Division, and the United States Army.

Murphy, Michael P.*

Rank and organization: Lieutenant, U.S. Navy SEAL. *Place and date:* Asadabad, Konar Province, Afghanistan, June 28, 2005. *Entered service at:* Pensacola, FL. *Born:* May 7, 1976, Smithtown, NY. *Date of issue:* October 22, 2007.

Citation: For conspicuous gallantry and intrepidity at the risk of his life above and beyond the call of duty as the leader of a special reconnaissance element with naval special warfare task unit Afghanistan on 27 and 28 June 2005.

While leading a mission to locate a high-level anti-coalition militia leader, Lieutenant Murphy demonstrated extraordinary heroism in the face of grave danger in the vicinity of Asadabad, Konar province, Afghanistan. On 28 June 2005, operating in an extremely rugged enemy-controlled area, Lieutenant Murphy's team was discovered by anti-coalition militia sympathizers, who revealed their position to Taliban fighters. As a result, between 30 and 40 enemy fighters besieged his four member team. Demonstrating exceptional resolve, Lieutenant Murphy valiantly led his men in engaging the large enemy force. The ensuing fierce firefight resulted in numerous enemy casualties, as well as the wounding of all four members of the team. Ignoring his own wounds and demonstrating exceptional composure, Lieutenant Murphy continued to lead and encourage his men. When the primary communicator fell mortally wounded, Lieutenant Murphy repeatedly attempted to call for assistance for his beleaguered teammates. Realizing the impossibility of communicating in the extreme terrain, and in the face of almost certain death, he fought his way into open terrain to gain a better position to transmit a call. This deliberate, heroic act deprived him of cover, exposing him to direct enemy fire. Finally achieving contact with his headquarters, Lieutenant Murphy maintained his exposed position while he provided his location and requested immediate support for his team. In his final act of bravery, he continued to engage the enemy until he was mortally wounded, gallantly giving his life for his country and for the cause of freedom. By his selfless leadership, courageous actions, and extraordinary devotion to duty, Lieutenant Murphy reflected great credit upon himself and upheld the highest traditions of the United States Naval Service.

Petry, Leroy A.

Rank and organization: Staff Sergeant, Company D, 2nd Battalion, 75th Ranger Regiment, U.S. Army. *Place and date:* Paktya Province, Afghanistan, May 26, 2008. *Entered service at:* New Mexico. *Born:* July 29, 1979, Santa Fe, New Mexico. *Date of issue:* July 12, 2011.

Citation: For conspicuous gallantry and intrepidity at the risk of his life above and beyond the call of duty.

Staff Sergeant Leroy A. Petry distinguished himself by acts of gallantry and intrepidity at the risk of his life above and beyond the call of duty in action with an armed enemy in the vicinity of Paktya Province, Afghanistan, on May 26, 2008. As a Weapons Squad Leader with D Company, 2nd Battalion, 75th Ranger Regiment, Staff Sergeant Petry moved to clear the courtyard of a house that potentially contained high-value combatants. While crossing the courtyard, Staff Sergeant Petry and another Ranger were engaged and wounded by automatic weapons fire from enemy fighters. Still under enemy fire, and wounded in both legs, Staff Sergeant Petry led the other Ranger to cover. He then reported the situation and engaged the enemy with a hand grenade, providing suppression as another Ranger moved to his position. The enemy quickly responded by maneuvering closer and throwing grenades. The first grenade explosion knocked his two fellow Rangers to the ground and wounded both with shrapnel. A second grenade then landed only a few feet away from them. Instantly realizing the danger, Staff Sergeant Petry, unhesitatingly and with complete disregard for his safety, deliberately and selflessly moved forward, picked up the grenade, and in an effort to clear the immediate threat, threw the grenade away from his fellow Rangers. As he was releasing the grenade it detonated, amputating his right hand at the wrist and further injuring him with multiple shrapnel wounds. Although picking up and throwing the live grenade grievously wounded Staff Sergeant Petry, his gallant act undeniably saved his fellow Rangers from being severely wounded or killed. Despite the severity of his wounds, Staff

Sergeant Petry continued to maintain the presence of mind to place a tourniquet on his right wrist before communicating the situation by radio in order to coordinate support for himself and his fellow wounded Rangers. Staff Sergeant Petry's extraordinary heroism and devotion to duty are in keeping with the highest traditions of military service, and reflect great credit upon himself, 75th Ranger Regiment, and the United States Army.

Pitts, Ryan M.

Rank and organization: Staff Sergeant, Chosen Company, 2nd Battalion (Airborne), 503rd Infantry Regiment, 173rd Airborne Brigade, U.S. Army. *Place and date:* July 13, 2008. *Date of issue:* July 21, 2014.

Citation: Sergeant Ryan M. Pitts distinguished himself by extraordinary acts of heroism at the risk of his life above and beyond the call of duty while serving as a forward observer in the 2nd Platoon, Chosen Company, 2nd Battalion (Airborne), 503rd Infantry Regiment, 173rd Airborne Brigade during combat operations against an armed enemy at Vehicle Patrol Base Kahler in the vicinity of Wanat Village, Kunar Province, Afghanistan, on July 13, 2008.

Early that morning, while Sergeant Pitts was providing perimeter security at Observation Post Topside, a well-organized anti-Afghan force consisting of over 200 members initiated a close-proximity sustained and complex assault using accurate and intense rocket-propelled grenade, machinegun, and small arms fire on Wanat Vehicle Patrol Base. An immediate wave of rocket-propelled grenade rounds engulfed the observation post, wounding Sergeant Pitts and inflicting heavy casualties. Sergeant Pitts had been knocked to the ground and was bleeding heavily from shrapnel wounds to his arms and legs, but with incredible toughness and resolve, he subsequently took control of the observation post and returned fire on the enemy. As the enemy drew nearer, Sergeant Pitts threw grenades, holding them after the pin was pulled and the safety lever was released to allow a nearly immediate detonation on the hostile forces. Unable to stand on his own and near death because of the severity of his wounds and blood loss, Sergeant Pitts continued to lay suppressive fire until a two-man reinforcement team arrived. Sergeant Pitts quickly assisted them by giving up his main weapon and gathering ammunition all while continually lobbing fragmentary grenades until these were expended. At this point, Sergeant Pitts crawled to the northern position radio and described the situation to the command post as the enemy continued to try to isolate the observation post from the main patrol base. With the enemy close enough for him to hear their voices and with total disregard for his own life, Sergeant Pitts whispered in the radio situation reports and conveyed information that the command post used to provide indirect fire support. Sergeant Pitts's courage, steadfast commitment to the defense of his unit, and ability to fight while seriously wounded prevented the enemy from overrunning the observation post and capturing fallen American soldiers and ultimately prevented the enemy from gaining fortified positions on higher ground from which to attack Wanat Vehicle Patrol Base. Sergeant Ryan M. Pitts's extraordinary heroism and selflessness above and beyond the call of duty are in keeping with the highest traditions of military service and reflect great credit upon himself, Company C, 2nd Battalion (Airborne), 503rd Infantry Regiment, 173rd Airborne Brigade and the United States Army.

Romesha, Clinton

Rank and organization: Staff Sergeant, 3rd Squadron, 61st Cavalry Regiment, 4th Brigade Combat Team, 4th Infantry Division, U.S. Army. *Place and date:* Kamdesh District, Nuristan Province, Afghanistan, October 3, 2009. *Entered service in:* California. *Born:* August 17, 1981, Lake City, CA. *Date of issue:* February 11, 2013.

Citation: For conspicuous gallantry and intrepidity in action at the risk of his life above and beyond the call of duty while serving as a Section Leader with Bravo Troop, 3rd Squadron, 61st Cavalry Regiment, 4th Brigade Combat Team, 4th Infantry Division, during combat operations against an armed enemy at Combat Outpost Keating, Kamdesh District, Nuristan Province, Afghanistan on October 3, 2009.

On that morning, Staff Sergeant Romesha and his comrades awakened to an attack by an estimated 300 enemy fighters occupying the high ground on all four sides of the complex, employing concentrated fire from recoilless rifles, rocket propelled grenades, anti-aircraft machine guns, mortars and small arms fire. Staff Sergeant Romesha moved uncovered under intense enemy fire to conduct a reconnaissance of the battlefield and seek reinforcements from the barracks before returning to action with the support of an assistant gunner. Staff Sergeant Romesha took out an enemy machine gun team and, while engaging a second, the generator he was using for cover was struck by a rocket-propelled grenade, inflicting him with shrapnel wounds. Undeterred by his injuries, Staff Sergeant Romesha continued to fight and upon the arrival of another soldier to aid him and the assistant gunner, he again rushed through the exposed avenue to assemble additional soldiers. Staff Sergeant Romesha then mobilized a five-man team and returned to the fight equipped with a sniper rifle. With complete disregard for his own safety, Staff Sergeant Romesha continually exposed himself to heavy enemy fire, as he moved confidently about the battlefield engaging and destroying multiple enemy targets, including three Taliban fighters who had breached the combat outpost's perimeter. While orchestrating a successful plan to secure and reinforce key points of the battlefield, Staff Sergeant Romesha maintained radio communication with the tactical operations center. As the enemy forces attacked with even greater ferocity, unleashing a barrage of rocket-propelled grenades and recoilless rifle rounds, Staff Sergeant Romesha identified the point of attack and directed air support to destroy over 30 enemy fighters. After receiving reports that seriously injured soldiers were at a distant battle position, Staff Sergeant Romesha and his team provided covering fire to allow the injured soldiers to safely reach the aid station. Upon receipt of orders to proceed to the next objective, his team pushed forward 100 meters under overwhelming enemy fire to recover and prevent the enemy fighters from taking the bodies of the fallen comrades. Staff Sergeant Romesha's heroic actions throughout the day-long battle were critical in suppressing an enemy that had far greater numbers. His extraordinary efforts gave Bravo Troop the opportunity to regroup, reorganize and prepare for the counterattack that allowed the Troop to account for its personnel and secure Combat Post Keating. Staff Sergeant Romesha's discipline and extraordinary heroism above and beyond the call of duty reflect great credit upon himself, Bravo Troop, 3rd Squadron, 61st Cavalry Regiment, 4th Brigade Combat Team, 4th Infantry Division and the United States Army.

Swenson, William D.

Rank and organization: Captain, 1st Battalion, 32nd Infantry Regiment, 3rd Brigade Combat Team, 10th Mountain Division, U.S. Army. *Place and date:* Ganjgal, Kunar Province, Afghanistan, September 8, 2009. *Entered service at:* Fort Benning, GA. *Born:* November 2, 1978. *Date of issue:* October 15, 2013.

Citation: For conspicuous gallantry and intrepidity at the risk of his life above and beyond the call of duty: Captain William D. Swenson distinguished himself by acts of gallantry and intrepidity at the risk of his life above and beyond the call of duty while serving as embedded advisor to the Afghan National Border Police, Task Force Phoenix, Combined Security Transition Command-Afghanistan in support of 1st Battalion, 32nd Infantry Regiment, 3rd Brigade Combat Team, 10th Mountain Division, during combat operations against an armed enemy in Kunar Province, Afghanistan on September 8, 2009.

On that morning, more than 60 well-armed, well-positioned enemy fighters ambushed Captain Swenson's combat team as it moved on foot into the village of Ganjgal for a meeting with village elders. As the enemy unleashed a barrage of rocket-propelled grenade, mortar and machine gun fire, Captain Swenson immediately returned fire and coordinated and directed the response of his Afghan Border Police, while simultaneously calling in suppressive artillery fire and aviation support. After the enemy effectively flanked Coalition Forces, Captain Swenson repeatedly called for smoke to cover the withdrawal of the forward elements. Surrounded on three sides by enemy forces inflicting effective and accurate fire, Captain Swenson coordinated air assets, indirect fire support and medical evacuation helicopter support to allow for the evacuation of the wounded. Captain Swenson ignored enemy radio transmissions demanding surrender and maneuvered uncovered to render medical aid to a wounded fellow soldier. Captain Swenson stopped administering aid long enough to throw a grenade at approaching enemy forces, before assisting with moving the soldier for air evacuation. With complete disregard for his own safety, Captain Swenson unhesitatingly led a team in an unarmored vehicle into the kill zone, exposing himself to enemy fire on at least two occasions, to recover the wounded and search for four missing comrades. After using aviation support to mark locations of fallen and wounded comrades, it became clear that ground recovery of the fallen was required due to heavy enemy fire on helicopter landing zones. Captain Swenson's team returned to the kill zone another time in a Humvee. Captain Swenson voluntarily exited the vehicle, exposing himself to enemy fire, to locate and recover three fallen Marines and one fallen Navy corpsman. His exceptional leadership and stout resistance against the enemy during six hours of continuous fighting rallied his teammates and effectively disrupted the enemy's assault. Captain William D. Swenson's extraordinary heroism and selflessness above and beyond the call of duty are in keeping with the highest traditions of military service and reflect great credit upon himself, Task Force Phoenix, 1st Battalion, 32nd Infantry Regiment, 3rd Brigade Combat Team, 10th Mountain Division and the United States Army.

White, Kyle J.

Rank and organization: Sergeant, Company C, 2nd Battalion (Airborne), 503rd Infantry Regiment, 173rd Airborne Brigade, U.S. Army. *Place and date:* Aranas, Afghanistan, November 9, 2007. *Entered service at:* Seattle, WA. *Born:* March 27, 1987. *Date of issue:* May 13, 2014.

Citation: Specialist Kyle J. White distinguished himself by acts of gallantry and intrepidity at the risk of his life above and beyond the call of duty while serving as a radio telephone operator with Company C, 2nd Battalion (Airborne), 503rd Infantry Regiment, 173rd Airborne Brigade, during combat operations against an armed enemy in Nuristan Province, Afghanistan, on November 9, 2007. On that day, Specialist White and his comrades were returning to Bella Outpost from a shura with Aranas village elders. As the soldiers traversed a narrow path surrounded by mountainous, rocky terrain, they were ambushed by enemy forces from elevated positions. Pinned against a steep mountain face, Specialist White and his fellow soldiers were completely exposed to enemy fire. Specialist White returned fire and was briefly knocked unconscious when a rocket-propelled grenade impacted near him. When he regained consciousness, another round impacted near him, embedding small pieces of shrapnel in his face. Shaking off his wounds, Specialist White noticed one of his comrades lying wounded nearby. Without hesitation, Specialist White exposed himself to enemy fire in order to reach the soldier and provide medical aid. After applying a tourniquet, Specialist White moved to an injured Marine, similarly providing aid and comfort until the Marine succumbed to his wounds. Specialist White then returned to the soldier and discovered that he had been wounded again. Applying his own belt as an additional tourniquet, Specialist White was able to stem the flow of blood and save the soldier's life. Noticing that his and the other soldier's radios were inoperative, Specialist White exposed himself to enemy fire yet again in order to secure a radio from a deceased comrade. He then provided information and updates to friendly forces, allowing precision airstrikes to stifle the enemy's attack and ultimately permitting medical evacuation aircraft to rescue him, his fellow soldiers, Marines and Afghan Army soldiers. Specialist Kyle J. White's extraordinary heroism and selflessness above and beyond the call of duty are in keeping with the highest traditions of military service and reflect great credit upon himself, Company C, 2nd Battalion (Airborne), 503rd Infantry Regiment, 173rd Airborne Brigade and the United States Army.

Iraq

Dunham, Jason L.*

Rank and organization: Corporal, 4th Platoon, Co. K, 3rd Battalion, 7th Marines (Reinforced), Regimental Combat Team 7, 1st Marine Division (Reinforced), U.S. Marine Corps. *Place and date:* Karabilah, Iraq, April 14, 2004. *Entered service at:* Scio, NY. *Born:* November 10, 1981, Scio, NY. *Date of issue:* January 11, 2007.

Citation: For conspicuous gallantry and intrepidity at the risk of his life above and beyond the call of duty while serving as a Rifle Squad Leader, 4th Platoon, Company K, 3rd Battalion, 7th Marines (Reinforced), Regimental Combat Team 7, 1st Marine Division (Reinforced), on 14 April 2004.

Corporal Dunham's squad was conducting a reconnaissance mission in the town of Karabilah, Iraq, when they heard rocket-propelled grenade and small arms fire erupt approximately two kilometers to the west. Corporal Dunham led his Combined Anti-Armor Team towards the engagement to provide fire support to their Battalion Commander's convoy, which had been ambushed as it was traveling to Camp Husaybah. As Corporal Dunham and his Marines advanced, they quickly began to receive enemy fire. Corporal Dunham ordered his squad to dismount their vehicles and led one of his fire teams on foot several blocks south of the ambushed convoy. Discovering seven Iraqi vehicles in a column attempting to depart, Corporal Dunham and his team stopped the vehicles to search them for weapons. As they approached the vehicles, an insurgent leaped out and attacked Corporal Dunham. Corporal Dunham wrestled the insurgent to the ground and in the ensuing struggle saw the insurgent release a grenade. Corporal Dunham immediately alerted his fellow Marines to the threat. Aware of the imminent danger and without hesitation, Corporal Dunham covered the grenade with his helmet and body, bearing the brunt of the explosion and shielding his Marines from the blast. In an ultimate and selfless act of bravery in which he was mortally wounded, he saved the lives of at least two fellow Marines. By his undaunted courage, intrepid fighting spirit, and unwavering devotion to duty, Corporal Dunham gallantly gave his life for his country, thereby reflecting great credit upon himself and upholding the highest traditions of the Marine Corps and the United States Naval Service.

McGinnis, Ross A.*

Rank and Organization: Private First Class, Company C, 1st Battalion, 1st Infantry Division, U.S. Army. *Place and date:* Adhamiya, Northeast Baghdad, Iraq, December 4, 2006. *Entered service at:* Pittsburgh, PA. *Born:* June 14, 1987, Meadville, PA. *Date of issue:* June 5, 2008.

Citation: For conspicuous gallantry and intrepidity at the risk of his life above and beyond the call of duty.

Private First Class Ross A. McGinnis distinguished himself by acts of gallantry and intrepidity above and beyond the call of duty while serving as an M2 .50-caliber Machine Gunner, 1st

Platoon, C Company, 1st Battalion, 26th Infantry Regiment, in connection with combat operations against an armed enemy in Adhamiyah, Northeast Baghdad, Iraq, on 4 December 2006. That afternoon his platoon was conducting combat control operations in an effort to reduce and control sectarian violence in the area. While Private McGinnis was manning the M2 .50-caliber Machine Gun, a fragmentation grenade thrown by an insurgent fell through the gunner's hatch into the vehicle. Reacting quickly, he yelled "grenade," allowing all four members of his crew to prepare for the grenade's blast. Then, rather than leaping from the gunner's hatch to safety, Private McGinnis made the courageous decision to protect his crew. In a selfless act of bravery, in which he was mortally wounded, Private McGinnis covered the live grenade, pinning it between his body and the vehicle and absorbing most of the explosion. Private McGinnis' gallant action directly saved four men from certain serious injury or death. Private First Class McGinnis' extraordinary heroism and selflessness at the cost of his own life, above and beyond the call of duty, are in keeping with the highest traditions of the military service and reflect great credit upon himself, his unit, and the United States Army.

Monsoor, Michael A.*

Rank and Organization: Petty Officer Second Class, SEAL Team 3, U.S. Navy. *Place and date:* Ar Ramadi, Iraq on September 29, 2006. *Entered service at:* Garden Grove, CA. *Born:* April 5, 1981, Long Beach, CA. *Date of issue:* April 8, 2008.

Citation: For conspicuous gallantry and intrepidity at the risk of his life above and beyond the call of duty as automatic weapons gunner for Naval Special Warfare Task Group Arabian Peninsula, in support of Operation Iraqi Freedom on September 29, 2006.

As a member of a combined SEAL and Iraqi Army Sniper Overwatch Element, tasked with providing early warning and stand-off protection from a rooftop in an insurgent held sector of Ar Ramadi, Iraq, Petty Officer Monsoor distinguished himself by his exceptional bravery in the face of grave danger. In the early morning, insurgents prepared to execute a coordinated attack by reconnoitering the area around the element's position. Element snipers thwarted the enemy's initial attempt by eliminating two insurgents. The enemy continued to assault the element, engaging them with a rocket-propelled grenade and small arms fire. As enemy activity increased, Petty Officer Monsoor took position with his machine gun between two teammates on an outcropping of the roof. While the SEALs vigilantly watched for enemy activity, an insurgent threw a hand grenade from an unseen location, which bounced off Petty Officer Monsoor's chest and landed in front of him. Although only he could have escaped the blast, Petty Officer Monsoor chose instead to protect his teammates. Instantly and without regard for his own safety, he threw himself onto the grenade to absorb the force of the explosion with his body, saving the lives of his two teammates. By his undaunted courage, fighting spirit, and unwavering devotion to duty in the face of certain death, Petty Officer Monsoor gallantly gave his life for his country, thereby reflecting great credit upon himself and upholding the highest traditions of the United States Naval Service.

Smith, Paul Ray*

Rank and Organization: Sergeant First Class, B. Company, 11th Engineer Battalion, 3rd Infantry, U.S. Army. *Place and date:* Baghdad, Iraq, April 4, 2003. *Entered service at:* Fort Leonard Wood, MO, October 1989. *Born:* September 24, 1969, El Paso, TX. *Date of issue:* April 5, 2005.

Citation: For conspicuous gallantry and intrepidity at the risk of his life above and beyond the call of duty.

Sergeant First Class Paul Ray Smith distinguished himself by acts of gallantry and intrepidity above and beyond the call of duty in action with an armed enemy near Baghdad International Airport, Baghdad, Iraq on 4 April 2003. On that day, Sergeant First Class Smith was engaged in the construction of a prisoner of war holding area when his Task Force was violently attacked by a company-sized enemy force. Realizing the vulnerability of over 100 fellow soldiers, Sergeant First Class Smith quickly organized a hasty defense consisting of two platoons of soldiers, one Bradley Fighting Vehicle and three armored personnel carriers. As the fight developed, Sergeant First Class Smith braved hostile enemy fire to personally engage the enemy with hand grenades and anti-tank weapons, and organized the evacuation of three wounded soldiers from an armored personnel carrier struck by a rocket propelled grenade and a 60mm mortar round. Fearing the enemy would overrun their defenses, Sergeant First Class Smith moved under withering enemy fire to man a .50 caliber machine gun mounted on a damaged armored personnel carrier. In total disregard for his own life, he maintained his exposed position in order to engage the attacking enemy force. During this action, he was mortally wounded. His courageous actions helped defeat the enemy attack, and resulted in as many as 50 enemy soldiers killed, while allowing the safe withdrawal of numerous wounded soldiers. Sergeant First Class Smith's extraordinary heroism and uncommon valor are in keeping with the highest traditions of the military service and reflect great credit upon himself, the Third Infantry Division "Rock of the Marne," and the United States Army.

Restoration of Award

In 1916, the War Department convened a panel to review the records of each Medal of Honor recipient. Upon review, 911 of these medals were canceled. In 1989, the U.S. Army Board of Correction of Records restored the medal to the following recipients.

Chapman, Amos

Rank: Civilian scout. *Born:* May 15, 1839, Kalamazoo, MI. *Organization:* Sixth U.S. Cavalry. *Place:* Washita River, TX. *Action Date:* September 12, 1874. *Date of issue:* November 4, 1874.

Citation: Gallantry in action. (In 1916, the general review of all MOHs deemed 900 unwarranted. This recipient was one of them. In June 1989, the U.S. Army Board of Correction of Records restored the medal to this recipient.)

Cody, William F.

Rank: Civilian scout. *Born:* Scott County, IA. *Organization:* Third Cavalry, U.S. Army. *Action date:* 26 April 1872. *Place:* Platte River, NE.

Citation: Gallantry in action. (In 1916, the general review of all MOHs deemed 900 unwarranted. This recipient was one of them. In June 1989, the U.S. Army Board of Correction of Records restored the medal to this recipient.)

Dixon, William

Rank: Scout. *Born:* 25 October 1850, Ohio County, WV. *War:* Indian Campaigns. *Organization:* Sixth U.S. Cavalry. *Place:* Wichita River, TX. *Action date:* September 12, 1874. *Issue date:* November 4, 1874.

Citation: Gallantry in action. (In 1916, the general review of all MOHs deemed 900 unwarranted. This recipient was one of them. In June 1989, the U.S. Army Board of Correction of Records restored the medal to this recipient.)

Doshier, James D.

Rank: Post guide during Indian Wars. *Born:* Warren County, TN, 2 May 1820. *Entered service at:* Fort Richardson, TX. *Place:* Holliday Creek TX, Little Wichita River. *ction date:* October 5, 1870. *ssue date:* November 19, 1879.

Citation: Gallantry in action and on the march. (In 1916, the general review of all MOHs deemed 900 unwarranted. This recipient was one of them. In June 1989, the U.S. Army Board of Correction of Records restored the medal to this recipient.)

Woodall, William H.

Rank: Civilian scout, U.S. Army, Major General Philip H. Sheridan's headquarters, during Civil War. *Birt date:* unknown. *Entered service at:* Winchester, Virginia. *Place and date:* Virginia, Appomattox campaign, Sailors Creek, March 29 to April 9, 1865. *Date of issue:* April 25, 1865. *Place:* Washington, DC, May 3, 1865. *ote:* Was chief civilian scout for Major General Philip H. Sheridan's Cavalry Corps, which consisted of VI and XIX Corps.

Citation: Was chief civilian scout for Major General Philip H. Sheridan's Cavalry Corps, which consisted of VI and XIX Corps. *Citation:* Captured flag of Brigadier General Rufus Barringer's headquarters brigade. (In 1916, the general review of all MOHs deemed 900 unwarranted. This recipient was one of them. In June 1989, the U.S. Army Board of Correction of Records restored the medal to this recipient.).

Renunciation of Award

Liteky, Charles

On July 29, 1986, Charles Liteky became the only known recipient to renounce his MOH. Liteky, a former Army chaplain, renounced his MOH in protest over U.S. policies in Central America.

For Additional Reading

CRS Report 95-519, *edal of onor: istor and ssues*, by David F. Burrelli and Barbara Salazar Torreon.

U.S. Congress. Senate Committee on Veterans Affairs. *edal of onor Reci ients* . Senate Committee Print No. 3. February 14, 1979. Washington, GPO. 1113 p.

———. *ietna Era edal of onor Reci ients* . Senate Committee Print No. 8. April 15, 1973. Washington, GPO, 236 p.

nited tates of erica s Congressional edal of onor Reci ients and eir Official Citations Columbia Heights, MN, Highland House II, 1996, 1119 p.

Contacts for Additional Information

Congressional Medal of Honor Society
Congressional Medal of Honor Society
40 Patriots Point Road
Mt. Pleasant, SC 29464
Telephone: (843) 884-8862
http://www.cmohs.org; medalhq@earthlink.net

The Congressional Medal of Honor Society was chartered by an act of Congress and signed into law by President Dwight D. Eisenhower. The purposes of the society are found in 35 U.S.C §33.

U.S. Army Human Resources Command, Awards and Decorations Branch
Adjutant General Directorate
https://www.hrc.army.mil/TAGD/Awards%20and%20Decorations%20Branch

Awards and Decorations Branch Related Links and Points of Contact (POC) at
https://www.hrc.army.mil/TAGD/
Awards%20and%20Decorations%20Branch%20Related%20Links%20and%20POCs

U.S. Army Medal of Honor:

http://www.army.mil/medalofhonor/

U.S. Army Center of Military History
Medal of Honor Citations
http://www.army.mil/cmh/moh.html

U.S. Army Total Personnel Command
Attn: TAPC PDA
Hoffman Building II
200 Stovall Street
Alexandria, VA 22332-0471
Telephone: (703) 325-8700
http://www.army.mil/medalofhonor/

U.S. Navy, Chief of Naval Operations (OPNAV09B33)
Navy Awards NO9B33
2000 Navy Pentagon
Washington, DC 20350-2000
Telephone: (202) 685-1770

U.S. Navy History and Heritage Command
Medal of Honor Recipients, Chronological Listing
http://www.history.navy.mil/photos/awd/us-indiv/moh-10.htm

U.S. Air Force Personnel Center
Attn: Awards and Decorations Branch
550 C Street West, Suite 12
Randolph AFB, TX 78150-4714
Telephone: (210) 565-2516

Commandant, U.S. Marine Corps
Attn: Military Awards Branch (MMMA)
Headquarters, U.S. Marine Corps

3280 Russell Road
Quantico, VA 22134-5100
Telephone: (703) 784-9206

Author Contact Information

Anne Leland

Information Research Specialist
aleland@crs.loc.gov, 7-4704